The Acrylic Artist's Bible

The Acrylic Artist's Bible

Marylin Scott

An essential reference for the practicing artist

CHARTWELL BOOKS

A QUARTO BOOK

Published in 2005 by
Chartwell Books
an imprint of Book Sales
a division of Quarto Publishing Group USA Inc.
142 West 36th Street, 4th Floor
New York, New York 10018
USA

ISBN-13: 978-0-7858-1944-8
ISBN-10: 0-7858-1944-4
QUAR.AABI

This book was designed and produced by
Quarto Publishing plc
The Old Brewery
6 Blundell Street
London N7 9BH

Project Editor Trisha Telep
Art Editor Tania Field
Designer Jill Mumford
Assistant Art Director Penny Cobb
Picture Researcher Claudia Tate
Photographer Martin Norris
Proofreader Louise Armstrong

Art Director Moira Clinch
Publisher Piers Spence

Manufactured by Provision
Printed in China by RR Donnelley

Contents

Introduction **6**

Choosing and using materials 8

Introducing acrylics **10**
Liquid acrylics **12**
Brushes **14**
Painting knives and paint shapers **16**
Palettes **18**
Painting mediums **20**
Interference colors **24**
Using thin paint **26**
Using thick paint **28**
Comparing methods **30**
Home-made canvas boards **32**
Stretching canvas **34**
Priming and staining **36**
Stretching paper **38**

Color 40

Primary colors **42**
Complementary colors **44**
Using complementary colors **46**
A basic palette **48**
Lightening and darkening colors **50**
Laying out and mixing colors **52**
Learning colors **54**
Mixing by glazing **56**
Using glazes **58**
Using a limited palette **60**
Mixing greens **62**
Mixing browns and grays **64**
Personal approaches **66**

Techniques 68

Basic techniques 70
Underdrawing **70**
Building up **72**
Blending **78**
Dry brush **80**
Spattering **82**
Scumbling **84**
Glazing **86**
Impasto **90**
Wet-in-wet **92**

Advanced techniques 94
Colored grounds **94**
Tonal underpainting **96**
Knife painting **98**
Extruded paint **100**
Stenciling **104**
Sgraffito **106**
Scraping **110**
Thin and thick contrasts **114**
Texturing the surface **118**
Wax resist **122**
Masking **126**
Monoprint **130**

Mixed-media techniques 134
Line and wash **134**
Pastel and acrylic **136**
Charcoal and acrylic **140**
Oil and acrylic **142**
Pencil and acrylic **144**
Watercolor and acrylic **146**
Collage **148**

Subjects 150

Landscapes 152
Trees **152**
Hills and mountains **156**
Water **158**
Tutorial: Acrylic and oil pastel **162**

Buildings 166
Urban scenes **166**
Individual buildings **170**
Interiors **172**

Still life 174
Shapes and textures **174**
Floral groups **176**
Tutorial: Using a restricted palette **180**

People 184
Portraits **184**
Figures in landscape **186**

Index **188**
Credits **192**

Introduction

Acrylic is the newest of all the painting mediums, having only been invented in the mid-20th century. It is widely used by professional artists, but is less popular with amateur painters, which is a pity, because it is a wonderfully versatile medium capable of achieving a vast range of different effects. It may be this very quality that puts people off—when there are so many possibilities, it can be hard to decide just how to start. But with *The Acrylic Artist's Bible* at hand, you have all the help and advice you will need—it's a must-have for anyone new to the medium, and even those who have used acrylic before will find some new ideas and inspiration.

The book is divided into four sections. The first, Choosing and Using Materials, contains helpful advice on the paints and equipment you will need to make a start, as well as providing tips on preparing your own boards and canvases. The second section, Color, explains some of the basic properties of color, showing ways of mixing colors, either on a palette or on the working surface, and provides essential advice on choosing a "starter palette."

▲ Learn about tools and materials

The third section, which forms the core of the book, presents the exciting range of techniques available to the acrylic painter. The chapter begins with a demonstration of three different ways of building up a painting from an initial sketch through to completion, so if you have not tried acrylics before, use these as your starting point. You will then be introduced to more unusual methods, all of which are fun to try out, so if you have not tried painting with knives, scratching into paint, squeezing paint on with an icing piper, building up exciting textures, or glazing over an underpainting, here is your chance. All the techniques are shown as a series of clear step-by-step

► Build a basic palette

◄ Discover new skills demonstrations done by a carefully selected group of professional artists, with captions explaining what to do at each stage. In the final section, Subjects, you will see the techniques in action. Finished paintings by a wide range of well-known acrylic painters illustrate the amazing diversity of styles possible with this wonderful medium, while text and captions provide hints on composition and uses of color. As an added bonus, there are two specially commissioned Tutorials, which enable you to follow an artist's progress from the planning of the picture through to completion. This section is intended to help you learn by example; looking at other people's work is an essential part of any artist's learning curve, and you may find that it helps you toward establishing your own style.

But the most important aspect to being an artist is to enjoy what you are doing, and to be willing to experiment with ideas and methods, so treat this book as a springboard to launch you into the exciting world of painting with acrylics.

► Look at paintings by established artists

1
Materials

Introducing acrylics

Acrylic paints are a by-product of the plastic industry, just like the latex paint we use on our walls. The pigments used for acrylics, with a few exceptions, are the same as those used for oils, watercolors and pastels; what makes them different is the binder, which is a polymer resin. This, once dry, acts as a form of plastic coating which cannot be removed.

Because the paints are water-based, they are thinned by mixing with water or with a combination of water and one of the many mediums specially made for the purpose (see page 20). With acrylics, you can paint in any consistency you like, which gives these paints what is perhaps their greatest virtue: amazing versatility. You can use them in thin washes resembling watercolor, or apply colors with a knife in thick slabs. You can use thick paint in one part of a picture and thin in another; you can build up an infinite variety of textures; and you can employ traditional oil-painting methods such as glazing—much easier in acrylic than in oil.

Painting sets

Several manufacturers offer introductory sets that include a range of pre-selected colors and, occasionally, different acrylic mediums, brushes, and palettes—all contained in either simple packaging or a tailor-made wooden box. These sets can be an expensive way to sample acrylics, and also the colors may not be to your liking, so it is usually better to purchase a few tubes and brushes separately.

Students' colors

Acrylics, like most other paints, are produced in two versions, students' and artists'. The former contain less pure pigment to the proportion of filler, making some of the colors slightly less intense, and the range of colors is smaller than the artists' colors. However, most are of very good quality, and being considerably less expensive than artists' colors, are ideal as an introduction to the medium.

Artists' colors

A selection from a range of artists' colors. This manufacturer produces a wide range of colors, all of which are classified as "flow-formula," which indicates that they are slightly runnier than some other paints.

Full-bodied paints

This manufacturer produces both "full-bodied" paints, shown here, and flow-formula. The thicker paints are best for oil-painterly effects.

Tube sizes

Some, but not all, manufacturers offer tubes in two or three sizes, with an extra large one (125ml) for white, which is used up very quickly. The smaller size (22ml) is an economical choice for expensive "special" colors that you don't use very often, such as reds, magentas and oranges.

Paint pots

Pots, which are usually slightly more fluid than tubed paints, are useful for large-scale studio work, but even the smaller sizes are less portable than tubes, so they are of limited use for outdoor sketching. If you do use them, avoid dipping the brush directly into the paint, as you will pollute the color if the brush is not perfectly clean.

Liquid acrylics

Liquid-acrylic color, which is slightly more expensive than tube acrylics, resembles ink or liquid watercolor. It is available in bottles with standard screw tops, and most bottle tops contain a dropper for transferring paint onto the palette. Liquid acrylics can be used in much the same way as ink and watercolor. Because they are made using an alkali resin, they can be softened and removed from pens and brushes with a preparatory alkali cleaning fluid.

These paints are good for painting in "watercolor mode," and work better than diluted tube colors. However, they are no substitute for true watercolor, and cannot be manipulated on the painting surface because they dry too fast.

Acrylic inks

Inks can be used in combination with acrylic paints, and are popular with artists using mixed-media approaches. The pearlescent inks shown here produce an attractive shimmering effect.

Acrylic inks

Bottles of liquid acrylics often contain a dropper that is used for transferring the paint onto the palette.

Medium-viscosity acrylic colors

Liquid acrylic colors

Chroma color

Chroma color is a type of water-based paint, originally developed for coloring cartoon cells. The colors are vibrant and strong. Made with acrylic resin, the paint can be used in a similar way to watercolor, gouache, ink, and, of course, acrylic itself. Chroma color is fast drying, waterproof when dry, and can be massively diluted without losing its strength of color. It can be mixed with special Chroma mediums to retard drying time and add thickness, gloss, or transparency (use of non-Chroma mediums is not advised). It is available in 80 different hues, packaged in 50ml tubes and bottles.

Tubes of Chroma colors

Bottled Chroma colors

Brushes

To a large extent, your choice of brushes will be dictated by the way you work—whether you apply the paint thickly or build up in thin layers. For thick applications and impasto work (see page 90), the bristle brushes made for oil painting are the best choice; while for watercolor styles and thin glazes (see page 86), you would use soft watercolor brushes. However, it is best to use the synthetic version of these, as sables could be spoiled by constant immersion in water.

Probably the best all-round brushes are those that are made specifically for acrylic work, as these combine the characteristics of both oil and watercolor brushes and can be used for medium to thick applications.

Nylon brushes

These brushes are made especially for acrylic work. They come in the standard brush shapes and a wide range of sizes, and are tough, hard wearing and springy.

1 *Small round nylon*
2 *Small flat nylon*
3 *Medium round nylon*
4 *Medium flat nylon*
5 *Large flat nylon*

Bristle brushes

These, which are usually made from hogs' hair, are the usual choice of artists who like to create oil-painterly effects.

6 *Medium bristle*
7 *Medium-large bristle*
8 *Large bristle*
9 *Small bristle*

Brush care

Because acrylic dries so fast, brushes must be kept wet throughout the working process, but don't leave them upside down in a jar of water for long periods, as this will splay the bristles. Stay-wet palettes (see page 18) have a special compartment for brushes, but if you don't have one of these, place the brushes flat in a shallow dish.

8

9

Brushes can very quickly become clogged with paint from the tip to the ferrule.

Before placing in water, remove the excess paint with a palette knife.

After each working session, rinse the brush in warm water and then clean by rubbing in into the palm of a soapy hand.

If the hairs have become splayed, reshape by dampening the brush and stroking it between finger and thumb.

Painting knives and paint shapers

Painting knives have a long history, as they have been used by oil painters for centuries, but they are especially well suited to acrylic work, as the paint dries fast enough to build up a painting in layers without disturbing the colors beneath. Painting knives are very sensitive implements, made of flexible steel and with cranked handles to hold the hand away from the work. They are made in a wide range of shapes and sizes, with each shape creating a distinctive mark of its own. Some artists use them as an alternative to brushes, while others restrict their use to highlights and accents in the later stages of a painting. Paint shapers look like traditional brushes, with wooden handles and chrome ferrules, but instead of holding bristles, they hold a flexible rubber tip. The tips come in both soft and firm rubber, and are available in a range of shapes and sizes. Pointed, round, chiseled, and angled ends move the paint around more in the manner of a palette knife than a brush. They are inexpensive, easy to clean and durable, and although brushes are better for some jobs, shapers make a range of distinctive marks, and are great fun to use.

Painting knives

Palette knife

Flat shaper
Interesting patterns can be made using a flat shaper.

Distinctive marks
A shaper can be used to make distinctive marks.

Flat shapers

*Pointed and
chisel-tipped shapers*

Palettes

Palettes for acrylic work must be a non-porous material such as plastic or glass, so don't try using the wooden palettes made for oil painting. Artists who work on a large scale often use sheets of glass, which can be easily cleaned, but if you do this, use heavy glass and tape the edges to prevent cuts. Pieces of laminated board can also be used, but they will become stained.

To prevent the paint from drying out, you can spray with water at regular intervals or use one of the special palettes designed for acrylic. These are made in two sizes, and are ideal for medium-thick paint applications, where you don't need to lay out large quantities of paint. They also have a compartment for brushes, which you fill with water.

Stay-wet palettes

These have been developed especially for acrylic, and can keep the paint wet for several days, or even weeks. They come in the form of a shallow tray with a clear lid, and are sold with a packet of two different types of paper. The absorbent paper is placed in the bottom of the tray and well wetted, and the membrane goes on top. The paint is laid out on the top sheet, and enough water seeps up to keep it moist. You can make your own "stay-wet" as shown on the next page.

Improvised palettes

Almost anything can be used as a palette—cans, glass jars, pieces of glass, large ceramic tiles, old plates and so on—and the paint can be covered with cling film to keep it moist when not in use.

The paint will remain damp for a very long time if sealed with plastic wrap.

Acrylic can be mixed on more or less any non-porous surface. Jars and other containers are useful if you want to mix large amounts of color.

Making a stay-wet palette

You will need a plastic or metal tray, a piece of capillary matting (as used by gardeners for keeping seed trays moist), same-sized pieces of drawing paper and either thin tracing paper or cooking parchment. You won't be able to make a lid, but you can use cling film instead.

1 Soak the capillary matting and place the drawing paper on top. An alternative is to use blotting paper instead of the matting, in which case you don't need the drawing paper.

2 Carefully place the tracing paper or cooking parchment on top, and you have your palette.

Tear-off palettes

You can buy disposable paper palettes, which you simply throw away after use, or you can use an old telephone directory, removing each sheet when it has become filled with paint.

Painting mediums

Although paint can be mixed with water alone, if you want to explore the full possibilities of acrylic you will need to become familiar with the appropriate mediums and find out what they do. The most commonly used mediums are matt and gloss, either of which is mixed with the paint to make it more thinner and transparent (the choice depends on whether or not you want a slight sheen). Gloss medium can also be used as a varnish, and matt medium is a useful primer for canvases (see page 32). Both are sold in bottles.

Retarding mediums

Retarding medium

This, which is sold in both tubes and containers, keeps the paint workable for longer, facilitating blending and wet-in-wet techniques. It is best used on its own, as water affects its performance. Take care not to work over a paint and retarder mix when it has become touch dry, as the surface becomes sticky and may be scuffed by subsequent brushwork.

Heavy gel mediums

These mediums are sold in both tube and pot form. They bulk out the paint but also increase its transparency, making it possible achieve exciting surface effects. They are usually mixed with water rather than being used on their own.

Heavy gel mediums

The effects of mediums

Those who have not used acrylics before may be surprised at how much the various painting mediums can alter the look and handling qualities of the paint. They offer exciting possibilities, but don't invest in a whole range until you have established your style and way of working, as they are fairly expensive.

Painting medium

This and the matt version are the standard painting mediums. They are usually mixed with water rather than being used on their own. Both matt and gloss mediums can also be used as varnishes to protect the completed work, but in this case, it is not necessary to add water. Varnishing finished work is not essential, but it can help to revive colors that have become dull.

Modeling pastes

These, sometimes called texture pastes, can be mixed with paint to thicken it, but are primarily intended for creating underlying textures over which thin paint is applied.

Texture paste

Resin sand texture gel

Light modeling paste

Modeling paste

Natural sand texture gel

Black lava texture gel

Texture pastes

Unlike modeling pastes, these are intended to be mixed with the paint to imitate a range of textures from sand and woodchips to glass beads. A range of different mediums are sold for bulking out paint. Texture pastes are made to resemble natural textures such as sand or fibers.

Glass bead texture gel

White opaque flakes texture gel

Blended fiber texture gel

continued on next page

Retarding medium is a must if you want to work wet-in-wet to achieve oil-paint effects, and for thick paint applications you may want to try one of the heavy gel mediums, which are sold in tubes. These bulk the paint while also making it more transparent, allowing for exciting effects.

Paint straight from the tube (left). Overlaid with iridescent medium (right).

Paint straight from the tube (right). Overlaid with matt medium (left).

Paint straight from the tube (left). Mixed with heavy gel medium (right).

Paint mixed with ceramic stucco, a texture paste.

Several other mediums are sold for impasto work (see page 90), among them being texture pastes and gels, and acrylic modeling paste, which is normally used for underlying textures. There are also "fun" mediums such as iridescent medium—which produces a range of metallic colors, and a special kind of reflective paint called interference colors—the effect of which is shown on page 24.

Paint mixed with resin sand, a texturing medium.

Paint mixed with blended fibers, a texturing medium.

Paint mixed with ceramic stucco, a texturing medium.

Paint mixed with natural sand, a texturing medium.

Interference colors

You may find it hard to believe, but these two paintings are in fact only one, seen in different lighting conditions. In *View of the Steens* William E. Shumway has stressed the changeable quality of the light by exploiting one of the most intriguing types of acrylic paint: interference colors. These are colorless, transparent paints made from titanium-coated mica flakes, and change their color according to the angle of viewing. As the light hits the flakes it either bounces off directly, reflecting the labeled color, or passes through another layer and bounces out at a different refractive index to display the complementary color. The colors can be applied straight from the tube, thinned with water or mixed with normal colors. Here, the artist has used them both as a transparent medium and for glazing over thick paint.

Rugged effects ▶
The light here has exposed a much more rugged effect, showing up strong darks in the mountains and foreground and an exciting range of blues and yellows in the sky.

Subtle contrasts ▶
In these lighting conditions, the tone and color contrasts in the sky are less obvious, but the blue of the hills shows up strongly.

Using thin paint

Acrylic paint can behave in similar ways to watercolor and oil paint, but it is a mistake to think of it as a poor man's version of either. It is an important medium in its own right, and has developed its own range of techniques.

Although flat and graded acrylic washes are made in exactly the same way as watercolor washes, and worked dark over light, they allow for more layers and more variations in the paint consistency than watercolors. Because the paint is stable once dry, there is no danger that overpainted washes will disturb or move previous washes. So, when using transparent methods, don't try to imitate watercolor—this is pointless. Instead, exploit the possibilities of acrylic to create its own unique effects.

Painting in watercolor mode

For this flower painting, the artist is using flow-formula paint (see page 10) with water but no addition of white, and using a soft-haired watercolor brush.

◀ *The completed painting is almost indistinguishable from an actual watercolor. Notice how the highlight whites have been achieved by reserving white paper rather than by using opaque white acrylic.*

Thin wash

Dilution with water or flow medium gives a transparent wash.

Granulation
Some colors granulate when water is applied. This occurs in watercolor also.

Graded wash
Adding water to the mix after each stroke creates a graded wash.

Adding white
The addition of white to the thin paint gives it a gouache-like quality.

Dark over light
The application of dark paint over dry, light paint results in a watercolor-like effect.

Glazing
Acrylic paint is excellent for glazing techniques; its quick-drying capacity enables the completion of a painting in one sitting. Use of transparent colors and a gloss medium will further increase the colors' brilliance and transparency. Complex color transitions can be built up effectively and easily. (See page 86 for more on this technique.)

Using thick paint

Used straight from the tube, acrylic paint has a buttery consistency. It can be moved and manipulated easily by brush or knife, and its character can be altered by the addition of various acrylic mediums (see page 20). Paint of this consistency is perfect for direct approaches, with even relatively thick paint drying within the hour. Gel medium can be added to preserve brush and textural marks. Blending, scumbling, and broken-color techniques all work well with paint of this consistency. For impasto work, use tube acrylic paint extended with a heavy gel medium, or with a texture medium or paste. Alternatively, you can create your own texture medium using additives like clean sand or sawdust (see pages 20 and 118).

Direct painting

Acrylic paint of a buttery consistency is perfect for more rapid applications.

Blending

Acrylic paint must be blended quite quickly, before it begins to dry.

Broken color

Areas of broken color can be built up relatively easily, as the paint dries quickly.

Scumbling

In this technique, a layer of wet paint is brushed over an initial dry, textured layer.

Texture mediums
Prepared texture mediums can be added to the paint to imitate a wide range of natural textures.

Making texture
Add fine sand to the paint for a textured look, but make sure the sand is clean.

Fork
Any household implement can be used to make impressions in impasto paint.

Tin foil
Crumpled tin foil pressed onto paint will give a stucco effect to your work.

Comparing methods

These two paintings show two very different uses of acrylic paint, one resembling an oil painting and the other looking more like a watercolor or gouache painting.

Oil-paint effects

Don Austen's *Barbara Hepworth's Greenhouse with Hanging Basket* was painted on canvas, with the paint built up thickly with energetic and varied brushmarks. In places, the paintwork looks a little like knife painting (see page 98) but, in fact, bristle brushes were used throughout.

Gouache effects

For this cool winter landscape painted on the spot on a small piece of card, Roy Sparkes began with paint diluted to a watercolor consistency, letting the colors merge wet-in-wet (see page 92) in the sky area and gradually thickening the paint toward the foreground.

◀ *In this detail, you can see the contrast of thin and thick paint. The area at top right has been built up with overlays of transparent color, as has the path on the left, but relatively thick paint of a gouache-like consistency has been used to suggest the highlights on the foliage.*

Home-made canvas boards

Suitable thin fabrics like canvas, hessian, muslin and calico can be glued to a board such as masonite to give it a textured surface. This method, called marouflaging, is an extremely inexpensive and effective way of using up fabric and off-cuts from boards, and results in a support that is excellent for use on location.

1 Rub the board thoroughly with a damp cloth to remove any dust, then place it face down onto the fabric. Cut the fabric to size, leaving a 2 in (50 mm) overlap on all four edges.

2 Turn the board face up and liberally paint the surface with a coat of acrylic matt medium.

3 Place the fabric square onto the board and brush on more medium. Start from the middle and work out to the edges, applying enough pressure to make sure no air bubbles or thick pockets of glue or medium are left. Continue until the fabric is completely flat.

4 When dry, turn the board over and place it on a block of wood. Apply acrylic matt medium around all four edges.

5 Fold the fabric over the sides and onto the back of the board. Smooth down using more acrylic matt medium. If the medium has raised the grain of the fabric, rub down lightly with glasspaper.

Stretching canvas

Stretching your own canvas is not only economical—it also allows you to prepare the canvas in accordance with your own specifications. Canvas is stretched over a frame made from mitred wooden stretcher bars, available from art stores in a range of lengths, widths and profiles—only stretcher bars of the same width and profile will fit together. Stretcher pieces are usually classified as economical, mid-quality, or professional quality, and are made from various species of kiln-dried pine or tulip wood. The highest-quality stretchers are jointed using a dovetail joint; others use a mortise and tenon. Many stretchers incorporate two slots into the corner joint to allow a triangular wooden wedge to be inserted; this can be used after priming to push the wood apart and apply lateral pressure to the canvas, stretching it taut.

1 Cut the canvas so that it is about 2 in (50 mm) larger than the stretcher frame. Assemble the stretcher, and check that it is square by measuring diagonally from corner to corner: if the measurements are the same, the frame is square.

2 Pull the canvas overlap up the sides and over onto the back of the stretcher frame. Secure at even 2 in (50 mm) intervals with staples.

3 Working one corner at a time, pull the corner of the canvas tightly across the back of the stretcher toward the center. Fold one of the canvas wings in and over.

4 Secure the fold to the stretcher frame using a single staple.

5 If the canvas remains limp when dry, it can be made taut by forcing the stretcher bars apart using wooden wedges hammered into the slots at each corner.

Priming and staining

Gesso gives an inflexible, slightly absorbent surface. Traditional gesso is made by mixing whiting with warm glue size and white pigment. (Black gesso is also available; another alternative is to tint acrylic gesso with black acrylic paint.) Acrylic gesso has one clear advantage over traditional gesso: it is flexible, and so it can be used on stretched canvas. Smooth boards are usually given several thin coats of gesso, with each coat painted at a right angle to the previous coat. Each coat is allowed to dry, and then sanded using fine-grit sandpaper before the next coat is applied. The number of coats required depends on the degree of surface smoothness desired.

1 Using a soft bristle brush, apply a layer of gesso to the surface of the board.

2 When the gesso is dry, sand the surface to remove any brushmarks.

3 Repeat steps 1–2 using brushstrokes painted at right angles to the previous ones. Always sand between coats.

Staining

Acrylic paint contains no corrosive ingredients that might degrade paper or fabric, making it possible to work directly onto canvas, without any prior sizing or priming. Acrylic paint applied to unsized canvas will soak into it, staining the fabric fibers; this stained layer can be sized and then worked on in a conventional manner, or worked on without sizing. Always work dark over light, allowing each stain to dry before applying the next. Too many stained paint layers will dull the colors. Raw canvas repels paint, while a flow medium added to a thin-color mix improves absorption. The support should be placed flat, or the thin paint will run. Once the paint has soaked into the fibers, it is impossible to remove, even when wet.

Flow medium has been added to the paint,
helping the canvas to absorb the color.

Priming and staining
Here you see how the unprimed canvas rejects the paint,
sitting on top of it rather than sinking in.

Stretching paper

When wetted, paper fibers absorb moisture like a sponge and swell, causing the paper to buckle. When the fibers dry, they shrink again—but not always to the original size—and the buckling can persist. The application of watery acrylic over such an uneven, "wavy" surface can be difficult. Stretching the paper helps to solve this problem by ensuring that the sheet dries flat each time it is wetted. You will need a sheet of paper, a wooden board that is larger than the paper, adhesive paper tape, a sponge, a craft knife and clean water.

1 Prepare four strips of adhesive-paper tape, cutting each strip approximately 2 in (50 mm) larger than the paper.

2 Lay the sheet of paper centrally on the wooden board and wet it thoroughly, squeezing water from the sponge. Alternatively, the paper can be wetted by holding it under a running tap, or by dipping it into water-filled tray or sink.

3 Wipe away any excess water with the sponge, taking care not to distress the paper surface.

4 Beginning on the longest side of the paper, wet a length of tape using the sponge, and lay it down along one edge. Ensure that about one-third of the tape surface is covering the paper, with the rest on the board.

5 Smooth the tape down with the sponge. Apply the tape in the same way along the opposite edge and then along the other two edges. Place the board and paper aside to dry for a few hours; or use a hairdryer to speed up the drying process, but keep the dryer moving so that the paper dries evenly, and do not hold it too close to the paper's surface.

ARTIST'S TIP

Staples can be used to secure medium- and heavyweight papers. Wet the paper and position it on the board, as above. Secure the edges by placing staples about ½ in (13 mm) in from each edge, and at ½–1 in (13–25 mm) intervals. Work quickly, before the paper buckles. Allow to dry as above.

2
Color

Primary colors

The three primary colors, so called because they cannot be mixed from other colors, are red, yellow and blue. A mixture of two primaries produces a secondary color: red and blue make purple; blue and yellow make green; yellow and red make orange. But there are many different reds, yellows and blues, and the secondary color obtained will depend on which ones are used. The tertiary colors are mixtures of three colors, that is, one primary and one secondary.

Creating secondaries

Pure secondaries are obtained by mixing primaries that show a bias toward one another on the color wheel. Subdued secondaries are created by mixing primaries that are further apart on the color wheel.

Pure secondary   Subdued secondary

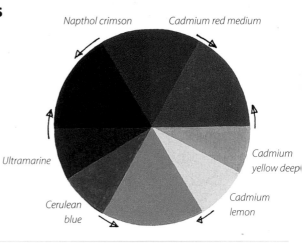

Napthol crimson   Cadmium red medium

Ultramarine

Cadmium yellow deep

Cerulean blue

Cadmium lemon

Mixing tertiaries

The tertiary colors are those that fall between the primaries and the secondaries. They are made by mixing equal amounts of a primary and the secondary next to it. The colors are red-orange, yellow-orange, yellow-green, blue-green, blue-violet and red-violet.

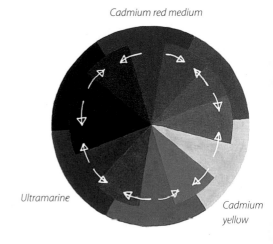

Cadmium red medium

Ultramarine

Cadmium yellow

Primary choices

In theory, you can mix all colors from only three—red, yellow and blue—but in practice it is not quite that simple, because there are different versions of these colors. In a limited palette, select two types of each, for example, cadmium red and crimson; cadmium yellow and lemon yellow, ultramarine and phthalo blue. Used in pairs, these give you many grades of secondary mixes—oranges, purples and greens—and by mixing two or more colors, you can obtain subtler shades and neutral colors. This chart shows a selection of these two-color mixes.

Basic color wheel *This six-color wheel shows the three primary colors and the secondaries made by mixing each of the primaries on either side. Simple wheels like this serve a valuable information purpose, but are of limited use when learning to mix colors, as they show only one version of each primary. However, you can see the position of the complementary colors, which play an important role in painting—these are explained on the following pages.*

Printer's wheel

Red: primary

Orange: secondary

Purple: secondary

Yellow: primary

Blue: primary

Green: secondary

Pigment wheel

Pigment color wheel *This wheel has been painted with acrylics, and shows two versions of each of the primary colors. Notice that they do not all correspond with the pure primary values of the printed wheel, as pigment colors are much more varied than those used for printing, and the color-mixing methods are different. The secondaries here show only one of many possibilities; you can make a much wider selection by varying the proportions of the primaries and by adding white, of course.*

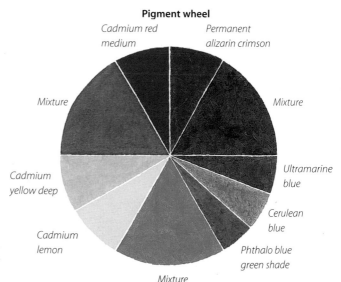

Cadmium red medium

Permanent alizarin crimson

Mixture

Mixture

Ultramarine blue

Cadmium yellow deep

Cerulean blue

Cadmium lemon

Phthalo blue green shade

Mixture

Complementary colors

Complementary colors are those that are opposite each other on the color wheel: orange and blue; red and green; violet and yellow. Good use can be made of these in painting. When juxtaposed, complementary colors create vibrant contrasts, while a color that looks too loud or bright can be "knocked back," or neutralized, by mixing in a little of its complementary. Another point to remember is that mixtures of complementary colors will produce neutral colors, so you can "knock back" a green that is too harsh by adding a little red, or vice versa.

Juxtaposing complementaries
Dynamic contrasts are created by putting complementary colors next to each other.

Orange

Blue

Red

Green

Violet

Yellow

Neutralizing colors *By mixing in a little of a color's complementary, brash colors can be "knocked back" and made more subtle.*

Mixing neutrals *A whole range of grays and browns can be created by using mixtures of complementary colors.*

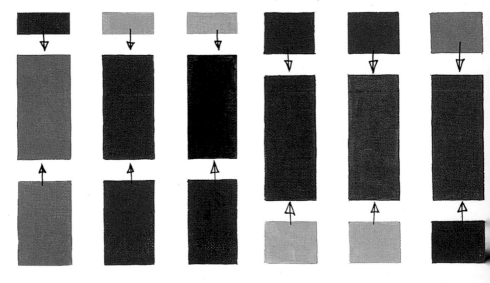

Optical mixing

The French painter Georges Seurat and others used to put small dabs or strokes of contrasting colors next to each other on the canvas, so that from a distance they would "mix" in the eye of the viewer. This method, called Pointillism, creates a lively impression, best appreciated at a distance so that "optical mixing" can take place. Versions of the technique are still used today. For the best results, the colors might be close in tone (i.e. of a similar lightness or darkness). Here are some examples:

White and red   Yellow   Orange

Black

White and green   White and purple   White and blue

Blue   White and purple   Green

White

Orange   Yellow   Red

Using complementary colors

Paul Powis has used the mauve/yellow complementary contrast very effectively in his painting, also bringing in subtle touches of the red/green contrast. His approach and method of execution are both very interesting. After working out a series of small sketches, he begins the painting proper on plywood that has been given a gloss black ground. Onto this, the shapes and elements are drawn in bright pastel before the paint is added.

▼ Using large brushes, the artist paints the complementary of the color he wants to end up with. In this case he wants a purple, and so the underpainting is done in yellow-orange.

◀ Working initially into the black ground, the colors are mixed very carefully until the tonal values are correct.

▲ The paint is worked wet-in-wet, using very direct and immediate brushstrokes.

Paul Powis
The Malverns
In addition to using heightened, non-naturalistic color, the artist has also combined semi-abstract shapes with realistic ones. The trees, although simplified, are clearly recognizable. However, the shapes in the foreground that lead the eye toward the focal point are not treated descriptively, because all that matters is the role they play in the composition.

A basic palette

When you are new to painting, it can be difficult to decide which colors to buy, as there are so many choices available. One way around this problem is to purchase one of the manufacturer's set of colors and add to them as and when you discover limitations. It is better—and more enjoyable—to select your own tubes. As long as you remember that you will need two of each of the primary colors (see page 42) you won't go far wrong. The suggested palette shown here adds a few extra colors to make 14 in total, including white. Those marked * are not strictly essential.

Titanium white *Strong and opaque. This is the only white available in acrylic ranges.*

Cadmium yellow deep *A strong, warm yellow tending toward orange, with good tinting strength.*

Cadmium red medium *Warm orangey-red, strong, and opaque, and with good tinting power.*

Yellow ocher * *Not strictly essential, as a similar color can be mixed, but worth including as it is often used.*

Alizarin crimson *A cool, slightly transparent red, good for glazes and in mixtures.*

Ultramarine *The best all-round blue, strong and warm. Tends to become dulled when mixed with white, but mixes well with other colors.*

Cadmium yellow lemon *A strong, acid yellow that mixes well with cool blues. Known by different names, but the word lemon always features.*

Phthalo blue *A very strong, greenish blue. Use with caution in mixtures, as it can overpower other colors. Also known as Winsor blue and phthalocyanine blue.*

Dioxazine purple * *A strong purple. Not strictly essential but is valued for its use in mixes.*

Raw umber *A dark greenish brown that leans toward gray when mixed with white. Useful all-round color.*

Phthalo green *Strong bluish green that makes a good base for mixing a range of cool greens. Viridian is an alternative, but is not as strong.*

Burnt sienna * *A strong red-brown that gives a surprising range of colors when mixed.*

Chromium oxide green * *An opaque, dull green that mixes well with other colors without overpowering them.*

Payne's gray * *Mixes well with other colors to produce dark tones without deadening them, and can also be used on its own. Some artists prefer black.*

Paint charts

All paint manufacturers produce color charts to help you make choices. These can be very useful, but bear in mind that printed and pigment colors always vary slightly.

Lightening and darkening colors

The obvious way to make colors lighter or darker is to add white and black (or gray) respectively, but this doesn't always work as it can change their hue. Black mixed with yellow, for example, makes green (worth remembering as this is a useful mixture), while white added to cadmium red results in a cool pink. Sometimes a better way of making a color lighter or darker is to add another one. For example, lemon yellow, which is pale in tone, can lighten one of the naturally dark reds, and yellow itself can be darkened by adding one of the browns. The chart opposite will give you some more ideas.

Overlaying colors

Colors can be lightened or darkened on the picture surface as well as by mixing in the palette. This can often create more exciting effects. The three examples below show darkening colors.

Dioxazine purple over alizarin crimson

Burnt sienna over lemon yellow

Burnt umber over cadmium red

Lightening by overlaying

These three examples show some alternatives for lightening colors. You can also, of course, use overlays of semi-transparent white.

Cerulean blue over ultramarine

Lemon yellow over burnt sienna

Yellow ocher over raw umber

Plus white	Plus black	Lightening colors	Darkening colors

Cadmium yellow — *Plus lemon yellow* — *Plus raw sienna*

Cadmium orange — *Plus lemon yellow* — *Plus alizarin crimson*

Alizarin crimson — *Plus cadmium red* — *Plus cobalt blue*

Windsor violet — *Plus permanent rose* — *Plus ultramarine*

Cobalt blue — *Plus cerulean blue* — *Plus ultramarine*

Cadmium green — *Plus lemon yellow* — *Plus chromium oxide green*

Laying out and mixing colors

Whether you use a large palette of colors or a small selection as shown here, always lay them out in some kind of logical order so that you can find them easily. One blob of dark color looks very much like another one, and it is very frustrating to find you have accidentally added green or brown to a blue sky mix. These colors are laid out from light to dark, with the color "families"—reds, blue and so on—grouped together. White can be placed at either end, but remember to lay out a larger quantity, as you will use more of this than the other colors (unless you are working in "watercolor mode").

Practicalities *This palette has been prepared for illustration purposes only. In reality, only lay out small quantities of acrylic color at a time, as they dry so rapidly. If you don't need a certain color, leave a space and add it later.*

Alizarin crimson

Cadmium red

Cadmium yellow

Phthalo blue

Ultramarine

Dioxazine purple

Lemon yellow

Raw umber

Payne's gray

Titanium white

Mixing on the palette

If you are using a stay-wet palette (see page 18) you will have to mix with a brush or you could damage the paper membrane. For large quantities of paint mixed on a rigid palette, such as a sheet of glass, you may find it easier to work the colors together with a palette knife. Knife mixing is especially useful if you are mixing your colors with a bulking medium for impasto work, as brushes will quickly fill up with paint and be difficult to clean.

Order of mixing *When mixing a pale color, start with the weakest ingredient, say yellow or white. Then add the stronger colors in small quantities, building up gradually to the strength you require. If you begin with a very strong hue you will have to add much more of the mixer colors, wasting a lot of paint.*

Knife mixing *Unless you want a streaky effect, which can be useful in certain cases, blend the colors together thoroughly. Don't just mash them together, as this can leave them partially unmixed; use the knife to scoop up the paint and knead the colors into one another.*

Brush mixing *This photograph shows what happens when thick paint is mixed with a brush. If a brush becomes overloaded with paint, act fast before it begins to dry. Lay the brush flat on the palette and run the edge of a palette knife or plastic card down the bristles from base to tip, then immerse the brush in water.*

Learning colors

Mixing colors is something that comes with practice, but the first skill that must be mastered is that of identifying the colors you see and thinking of them in terms of the paints on your palette. Anyone can describe a color in its most basic terms—even small children can see that something is red, yellow or blue—but deciding what kind of color it is is more difficult, especially in the case of neutral colors, which often don't seem to fit into any clear category. But even neutrals have some kind of color bias: gray can be blue-gray or green-gray, while browns range from near-reds to greenish yellows.

So when you look at something, try to think your way through the following checklist of points, which will give you a clue as to the ingredients of your mix.
• What kind of color is it?
• Is it light, mid-toned or dark?
• Which of my tube colors is nearest to it?
• Does it have a distinct tinge of another color?
• Is it warm or cool?
• Is it intense or subdued?

The color swatches below show examples of how these principles can be applied.

Modifying colors

One of the things that often goes wrong with color mixing is that the color looks right on the palette and wrong when you paint it on. This is because colors don't exist in isolation; their individual identity derives from their relationship with other colors. A neutral color that looks relatively dull on the palette can appear quite vivid and glaring if it is painted in among other even more subdued colors, and its color bias will become much more obvious. Similarly, a bright color may become dulled unless it is contrasted with neutrals or with darker or lighter tones. Color is full of surprises, sometimes unhappy ones, but in acrylic it is very easy to modify colors, either by overpainting or by glazing (see page 86).

Warm	Cool	Dark	Light	Color bias
Cadmium red + black + white	Phthalo green + black + white	Dioxazine purple + phthalo green	White + lemon yellow + black	Lemon yellow (+ raw umber + white)
Cadmium yellow + white + dioxazine purple	Dioxazine purple + raw umber + white	Ultramarine blue + napthol crimson	White + dioxazine purple + cadmium yellow	Ultramarine blue (+ raw umber + white)

Modifying hues

Some acrylic colors are very strong and artificial-looking and are not always suitable for painting natural subjects. If you want to modify a hue quite subtly, try adding small touches of subdued earth colors—the muted browns and yellows. For example, mix burnt sienna into green, and yellow ocher into mauve.

Bright green

Bright green with burnt sienna added

Bright green mixed with red-violet

MIXING COLORFUL NEUTRALS

Neutral colors need not be dull, and it is worth experimenting with different ways of mixing them. One easy and quick method is to mix complementary, or opposite, colors such as red and green (see page 44). The kind of mixture you achieve depends on the proportions of the mix. The same method can be used to modify colors, either by glazing or by adding a little of the opposite color to the palette mixture.

Knocking back colors

If one color in your painting looks too bright, lay a thin, neutral-colored glaze over it, using a large, soft brush and paint mixed with either water alone or a mixture of water and acrylic medium (see page 20). Colors that are either too light or too dark in tone can be modified in the same way with darker or lighter versions of the original color, or with very thin white or gray.

1 *A vivid purple, diluted with water, is laid over dry paint.*

2 *The effect was found to be over-bright, so it is modified with glazes of a more subdued hue.*

3 *The finished effect is still bright due to the strong contrasts, but the purple is slightly more subtle.*

Mixing by glazing

A glaze is a transparent layer of paint applied over another color so that it tints and modifies the underlayer. Any number of glazes can be superimposed as long as each is allowed to dry before painting the next. Glazing was originally an oil-painting technique, but is ideal for fast-drying acrylics, and the effects are quite unlike those simply achieved with opaque mixtures.

Mixing and glazing—comparing the effects

1

3

2

4

1 Deep violet mixed with cadmium yellow lemon; **2** Cadmium yellow lemon glazed over deep violet; **3** Medium magenta mixed with light emerald green; **4** Medium magenta glazed over light emerald green

Cadmium red

Cadmium orange

Naphthol crimson

Cadmium yellow lemon

Phthalo green

Phthalo blue

Medium magenta

Raw umber

Payne's gray

Unbleached titanium

▼ The horizontal bands of color have been laid over the vertical ones. Notice that the degree to which the colors are amended depends on the tone and relative opacity of the pigment.

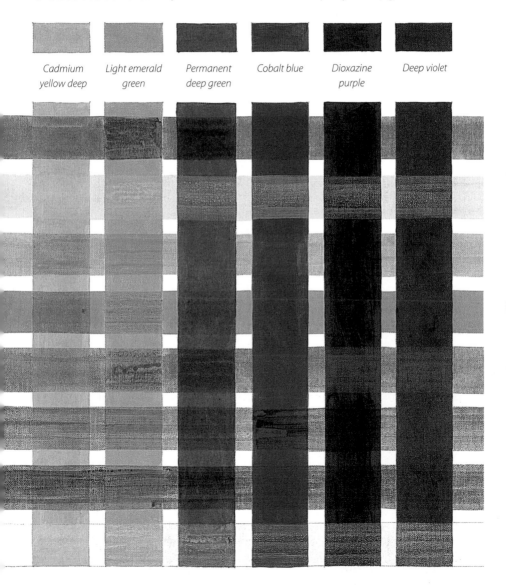

Cadmium yellow deep

Light emerald green

Permanent deep green

Cobalt blue

Dioxazine purple

Deep violet

Using glazes

This painting, done on smoothly primed board, shows the depth and intensity of color that can be achieved by glazing. A detailed pencil drawing was made before washing over the board with a yellow oxide and white mix. The landscape was developed with orange and purple washes, allowing each previous layer to show through. The figure of the girl was worked in much the same way, but with more layers of thicker paint to give her an impression of solidity.

▲ The texture of rock and sand was achieved by loosely scrubbing on the paint with a bristle brush. This causes the paint to froth. When dry, the shapes of the bubbles are visible, with subsequent layers exaggerating the effect. A cadmium yellow and naphthol crimson mix make up the base color for the rocks, with naphthol crimson and cobalt blue added by degrees for the areas in shadow.

▲ The purple of the pyramids consists of Payne's gray, naphthol crimson and titanium white. Although the color scheme is essentially warm, the coolness here helps to suggest distance.

▲ The darker hair was painted first with a mix of yellow ocher, Payne's gray and titanium white. When dry, masking tape was put onto the hair area and the light wisps of hair cut out; these were then painted with a thick mixture of cadmium yellow and titanium white.

Ian Sidaway
The Sphinx, the Pyramids and Alice at Giza

◀ *The skin tones were obtained by using the same combination of colors used on the rocks with the addition of yellow oxide and white for the highlights.*

Using a limited palette

The chart below shows how a large range of colors can be achieved with only eight basic hues. The horizontal band of swatches has been mixed with the vertical band in a ratio of 20:80, and changing the ratio will give an even wider selection.

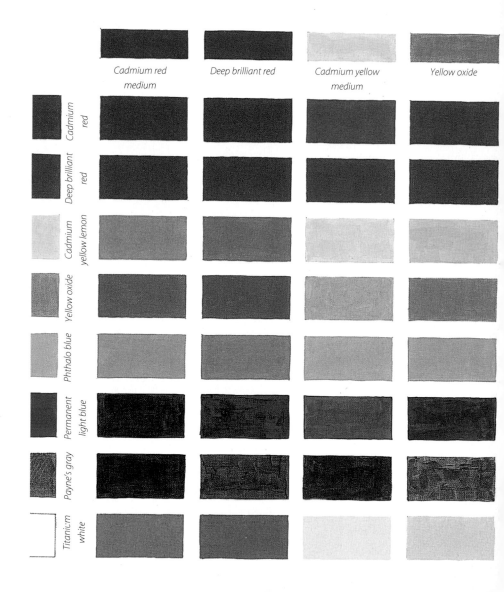

Permanent light blue · Phthalo blue · Payne's gray · Titanium white

Cadmium red

Deep brilliant red

Cadmium yellow lemon

Yellow oxide

Phthalo blue

Permanent light blue

Payne's gray

Titanium white

Mixing greens

Greens vary hugely in nature, but many beginners fail to mix a satisfactorily wide range. This chart should provide some ideas. Each group of three swatches shows: top = 50:50 pure mix, center = white added to top swatch, bottom = white added to center swatch.

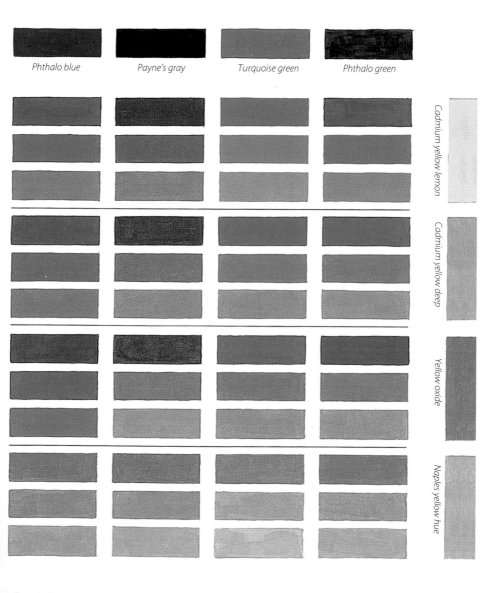

Phthalo blue Payne's gray Turquoise green Phthalo green

Cadmium yellow lemon

Cadmium yellow deep

Yellow oxide

Naples yellow hue

Mixing browns and grays

This chart shows that many of the so-called neutral hues are actually quite colorful. Each group shows: top = 50:50 pure mix, center = top swatch with white added, bottom = center swatch with white added.

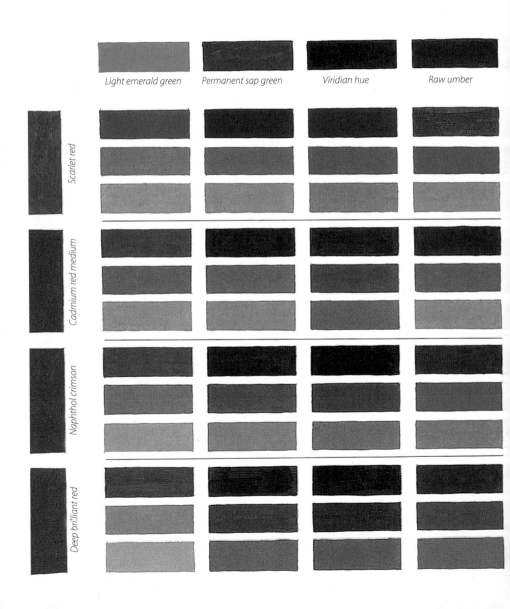

Light emerald green   Permanent sap green   Viridian hue   Raw umber

Scarlet red

Cadmium red medium

Naphthol crimson

Deep brilliant red

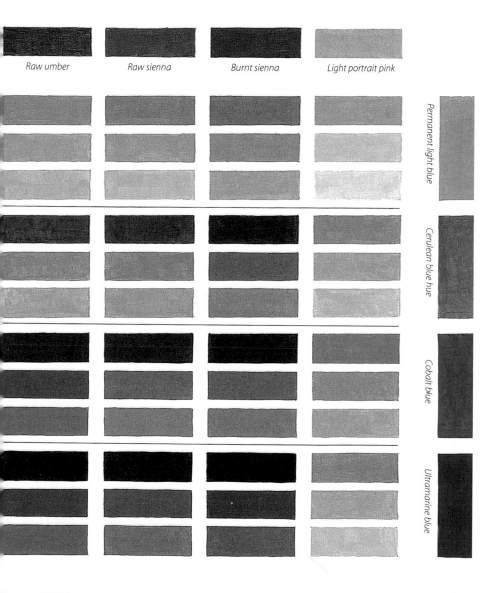

Raw umber   Raw sienna   Burnt sienna   Light portrait pink

Permanent light blue

Cerulean blue hue

Cobalt blue

Ultramarine blue

Personal approaches

Learning to mix colors is a basic skill like any other, but using color is a vital part of the artistic process, and your choice of colors gives you a means of self-expression. Many artists' work is immediately recognizable by the personal palette they use, which tends to be similar whatever their subject matter.

Peter Burman
River Deben, Suffolk
In dramatic contrast to Gerry Baptist, this artist has muted his colors where necessary and brought in blue-grays to contrast with the pale yellows of the sunlit fields. This painting is about light. Notice that only the most subtle and dulled-down greens have been used for the trees, as any vivid greens would have stood out too much and detracted from the drama of the stormy sky.

◀ **Gerry Baptist**
Pines in a Clandon Garden
This artist enjoys using heightened color whether he is painting landscape, still life, or portraits, and his painting has a jewel-like quality reminiscent of the paintings of Matisse and the Fauve painters. Although the colors are not realistic, there is nothing arbitrary about their use, and each one is carefully mixed on the palette before applying. The only neutral color used in this painting is the blue-gray of the sky, which helps the brilliant reds and blue-greens to sing out.

3
Techniques

Underdrawing

It is not essential to draw before you paint, but it is wise to do so if your subject is at all complicated or involves hard-to-draw elements, such as figures. If you are using opaque techniques, the paint will completely cover your drawing, so you can draw in whatever medium you like—pencil, charcoal, or a brush and thinned paint—though charcoal is best avoided if you intend to start with pale colors, as it can muddy them slightly.

Transparent techniques need more planning, as heavy lines may show through the washes, particularly in very light areas. So keep the lines as light as possible, avoiding shading, and don't start to paint until you are sure the drawing is correct.

1 A light pencil drawing like this is best for transparent watercolor-style applications.

2 If a stronger drawing is needed, light washes can be laid over the pencil drawing in the areas which are to be darker in the painting.

3 For more opaque techniques and bolder treatments, a brush drawing is the most common method. If any lines threaten to show through, they can be overpainted in white.

Building up

The way you proceed with a painting in acrylics depends to a large extent on your individual working method and on how you are using the paint—thick, thin or medium. If you are exploiting transparent techniques on paper, you will want to begin with light washes of color, building from light to dark in the traditional watercolor manner.

For opaque treatments, it doesn't matter where you begin or which colors you put down first, because you can overpaint as much as you like without harming the colors beneath.

A good general rule is to block in the most important areas of tone and color first and then work all over the picture at the same time, always bearing in mind the relationships between the various shapes, tones and colors. The following pages show three different approaches.

Medium consistency paint on paper

1 Working on watercolor paper with a medium (slightly textured) surface, this artist first made an outline-brush drawing and now lays in color, using water-thinned paint for the carafe to simulate the transparency of the glass. Although the glass has a greenish tinge, it reflects the color of the background, so a warm brown is chosen.

2 The subtle colors of the glass have been built up with a series of transparent washes, while thicker paint, applied with a bristle brush, has been used for the highlights on the carafe. The same paint is used to work into the dark area on the right.

3 The background is strengthened with a thicker application of paint. Using a nylon brush, which is better for precise definition than a bristle one, the artist takes the color around the edges of the cork and the handle of the carafe.

4 Thicker paint is used for the highlight on the side of the glass. Because it threatens to overlap the edge, the artist pushes it into place with her finger.

5 In order to achieve the elusive quality of the glass carafe, a glaze of transparent greenish yellow is laid over the original browns and whites. The glaze is applied with a large, soft brush, and the paint is thinned with water alone.

6 The finished painting shows how the consistency of the paint can be varied to suit the subject. On both of the glass objects, opaque highlights overlay transparent washes, while relatively thick paint has been used for the drapery.

Thick paint on canvas

1 The artist began with a careful drawing in water-thinned paint. His preferred medium is oil paint, and he uses the same techniques for acrylic, beginning with fairly thin but opaque paint and building up gradually.

2 He establishes all the main color areas first, working broadly and attempting no precise definition, although he takes care to keep within the lines of his original drawing.

3 A variety of colors has been used for the body of the carafe, and three separate colors for the dark parts of the rim and handle.

4 The glass is now fully defined, the tricky ellipse at the top having been treated with care. The final stage, often one of the most enjoyable in a painting, is adding the highlights, which bring the whole image to life.

5 Thick paint, varied brushwork, and carefully orchestrated colors give a lovely feeling of energy to the subject, and the transparency of the glass is skillfully conveyed.

Transparent paint on paper

1 As in the demonstration on page 72, the artist is working on watercolor paper. She has made no underdrawing because she intends to use transparent paint throughout, and pencil or brush lines could show through in the light areas. She begins with very pale washes, building up gradually toward the darks by laying one wash over another. Using acrylic in this way requires considerable skill, as mistakes cannot be corrected by overpainting.

2 At this stage, the painting gives the impression of a ghost image. Certain colors will be strengthened as the work progresses, while others will be left as they are.

3 Due to the effects of light, the contrasts of tone on glass objects can be strong, with abrupt transitions from light to dark. Here, a dark green is used for the rim and handle of the carafe. The paint is still of watercolor consistency, although there is now a higher ratio of paint to water.

4 Further washes of watery paint are applied to the body of the carafe, building up the effect of the wavy light and dark areas caused by inconsistencies in the thickness of the glass.

5 The finished painting has all the delicacy and translucency of a watercolor, though the color has a slightly grainier consistency.

Blending

Blending means merging one color or tone into another so that there are no perceptible boundaries between them. Because acrylic dries fast and thus can only be manipulated on the painting surface for a short time, it lends itself less readily to blending techniques than other paints, but it can be done.

The thicker you use the paint, the longer it will stay wet, making blending easier, but you can prolong the drying time even further by adding retarding medium to the colors as you mix them (see page 20). This will allow you to "push" one color into another. Blending can also be done by the dry-brush method shown on the following pages; laying down an area of flat color and then working over it with a small amount of paint on a bristle brush.

1 The eggplant is painted first. The paint has been mixed with retarding medium, and remains wet for long enough to blend one color into another with a finger.

2 Painting the darkest and lightest areas of the eggplant first helped the artist to judge the strength of color needed for the red bell pepper, which was initially blocked in with brushstrokes following the forms. Again a finger is used to blend one color into another.

3 Further dark colors are applied to the eggplant. A nylon brush is used throughout, as this is softer than a bristle brush, and does not leave pronounced brushmarks.

4 Yellow was added to the basic red mixture for the pepper and applied gently onto the side. The retarding medium makes the paint more transparent so that new applications do not completely cover the underlying colors. The highlights, which do not need to be blended, are added with less medium added to the paint.

5 The brushmarks are barely visible, and there is no obvious boundary between each color and tone. Although retarding medium is helpful, it needs to be used with caution. On a non-absorbent surface such as primed canvas board, the paint remains tacky for some time, and there is a danger of accidentally lifting off small areas of color.

Dry brush

Dry brush is a technique common to all the painting media, whether opaque or transparent. It simply means working with the minimum of paint on the brush so that the color below is only partially covered.

You can work dry brush straight onto virgin paper or canvas, but it is more usual to work it over a previously laid color, thus achieving a broken-color effect.

For thin acrylic, you will need to use a soft brush, ideally a square-ended one, with the hairs splayed out slightly. Experiment on a spare piece of paper beforehand; it is important to get exactly the right amount of paint on the brush or it will go on too heavily and spoil the effect.

If the painting is in thick or medium-thick acrylic it is probably best to use a bristle brush—the fan-shaped ones sold as "blending brushes" are useful. You can brush equally thick, fairly stiff paint over the underlayer, or use thin paint over thick, depending on the effect you want to achieve.

1 The artist is working on canvas, and begins by giving it an overall tint (see page 37), spreading well-diluted paint with a piece of kitchen paper.

2 Working with a bristle brush, he drags thick paint lightly over the canvas so that some of the warm undercolor shows through.

3 The texture of the crusty loaf is accurately represented by successive applications of dry brush. Because acrylic dries so fast, one layer of paint can be laid over another almost immediately.

4 The edge at the top of the loaf is crisp and clear, so here juicier paint is used, and applied more heavily.

5 On the bread board, considerable variations of color and tone have been achieved by laying one color over another. The dry-brush method is again used for the soft, broken line of shadow beneath the loaf.

6 Dry brushing is an excellent method of suggesting texture, and has also allowed the artist to build up subtle but lively interactions of color.

Spattering

Spraying or flicking paint onto the picture surface is an excellent way of suggesting certain textures, and can also be used to enliven an area of flat color—perhaps in the background of a still life. Watercolor-landscape painters sometimes use spattered paint to convey the crumbly appearance of cliffs and sandy beaches, or spatter opaque white paint to describe the fine spray of a breaking wave.

An old toothbrush is the implement most commonly used for spattering. You can also use a bristle brush, which makes a coarser spatter with larger droplets of paint. Or, for a really fine spatter over a large area, use a plant spray or a spray diffuser of the type sold for use with fixative. In this case, you would need to mask any areas of the work that are to remain free of sprayed paint.

Whichever method you use, it is important to remember that spattered paint frequently lands in the wrong place—on your clothes, the floor and walls, and your work table—so it is essential to protect all vulnerable surfaces.

1 The landscape is blocked in simply, with little detail in the foreground, as this will be built up with spattered paint.

2 A piece of newspaper is placed over the area to be kept free of spatter. More elaborate masks, made from torn strips of newspaper, are also positioned. Red paint is then flicked on using the side of a large brush, which produces a coarse spatter with quite large droplets of paint.

3 The effect can be softened by blotting with newsprint or other absorbent paper. In this case, blotting also produces variations in size, as the paper spreads out the wet droplets.

4 The bush in the middle distance is next to be spattered, again after masks have been placed around the area. Because the bush is farther away, the spatter needs to be less obtrusive, so a toothbrush is used, which releases finer particles than a paintbrush. Load it with paint that is well thinned but not too watery, and quickly draw your thumb across the bristles.

5 As a final touch, the bush was spattered again with light yellow-green and again blotted with paper to merge the drops. The layers of light-brown and bright-red spatter in the foreground suggest flowers and grass very effectively.

Scumbling

This method involves scrubbing an uneven layer of paint over an existing color.

Whether you choose to scumble a contrasting color or a similar one depends on the effect you are seeking. You might, for example, scumble several subtle colors over a base coat of mid-gray to suggest the texture of a stone wall, or you might enrich a vivid color, such as a deep, bright blue, by scumbling over it with shades of violet or lighter blue. The most important thing to remember is that you should not cover the color beneath completely, so the paint is usually applied with a light scrubbing action—using a stiff brush, a rag, or even your fingers. If you are working on canvas or canvas board, the grain will help you, because the paint will be deposited only on the top of the weave, but scumbling can also be done quite effectively on a smooth surface such as primed masonite (see page 32).

1 An underpainting of relatively flat color has been made on watercolor paper, and the artist uses a bristle brush to dab and scrub light, opaque paint over the darker color to produce a veil-like effect.

2 After the first layer of scumbling at the top of the picture, the composition has been defined with lines of light colored paint. In the foreground, dark red-brown is scumbled over the green.

3 Scumbling is an imprecise method, impossible to restrict to a small area, so before turning her attention to the sky, the artist has protected the area by covering it with tape.

4 The tape is removed to leave a crisp edge. Masking (see page 126) is extremely useful for techniques such as scumbling and spattering.

5 Masking tape was also used to protect the margins of the paper. This results in a perfectly defined straight edge which complements the edge qualities in the painting and contrasts with the soft broken-color of the scumbling method.

Glazing

This is a technique first used in the early days of oil painting, when paint was built up in a series of transparent or semi-transparent layers over an underpainting. Each layer must be dry before the next is applied, so the method is perfect for fast-drying acrylics. The effect of successive veils of color is quite unlike anything you can achieve with opaque paint, and glazing allows you to build up colors of great depth and richness.

Glazing can be done with paint thinned with water alone, but the colors will be more vivid and more transparent if you use a mixture of water and acrylic medium—either matt or gloss. The layers need not all be uniformly thin; you can glaze a thin layer over impasto, or over an area in which you have built up a heavy texture with modeling paste.

1 Working with a soft brush on watercolor paper, the artist has begun with thin washes of yellow over a pencil drawing. She now mixes the paint with a little matt medium and applies it more thickly.

2 The paint is mixed with matt medium throughout, as the picture is to be built up with successive layers of glazes. Notice that the medium makes the paint more transparent.

3 Several layers of semi-transparent color have begun to establish the form of the plums, and delicate touches of darker color are now applied to suggest the texture of the lemon.

4 A deep, rich purple red is used for the dark area of shadow where the fruit turns away from the light.

Continued on next page

5 For the plum in the foreground, more blue is added to the crimson, producing a very deep but still transparent color that allows the red to show through.

6 The matt medium reduces the "body" and opacity of the white paint, making it ideal for suggesting the light bloom on the plum. The paint is gently pulled over the paper surface in a scumbling method.

7 The effect produced by this layering technique is very distinctive, with one color showing through another to achieve subtle and glowing mixes. You can see this particularly clearly on the plums, and on the shadows beside them.

Impasto

The word impasto describes paint applied thickly enough to hold the marks of the painting implement.

Impasted paint can be applied with a brush or a painting knife, or even squeezed onto the painting surface. You can use thick paint all over the picture surface, as Van Gogh did, or reserve it for certain areas. In a still life you might use thin layers of paint for the background and any shadows on the objects, and touches of impasto for highlights or areas of vivid color.

If you plan large areas of thick paint, you will find it helpful to mix the colors with one of the mediums made for the purpose (see page 20). Some of these bulk out the paint without changing its color, while others make it more transparent. When using impasto mediums, remember that the palette mixture will dry slightly darker because the mediums are white when wet and colorless when dry.

Impasto under glazing

1 Working on primed canvas board, thick paint is applied with a bristle brush over a slightly thinner layer. The paint has been thickened with impasto medium in an approximately 50:50 mixture.

2 In places, the handle of the brush was used to "model" the thick ridges of paint and push them into place. The paint has also been scratched into with the point of a painting knife.

3 A glaze of water-thinned paint is now applied, creating blobs and runnels where it catches on the impasted paint. Any unwanted drips can be mopped up with a rag.

Using gel medium

David Alexander paints large-scale works on canvas, and thickens his paint with a heavy gel medium. Like many painters who exploit the tactile qualities of really thick paint, he employs various unorthodox painting "tools," among them scrapers, sponges, and hardened brushes. In *The Sun's Recoiled Glare* you can see a contrast of surface textures, with thick swirls of paint in places and sgraffito effects (see page 106) in others.

Using the paint consistency

In *Lavender Fields, Provence*, Peter Burman uses paint straight from the tube, that is, not thickened with any medium. Often thick impastos are reserved for foreground details but in this case the blue fields have been generalized in order to give prominence to the sunlit group of buildings, which are skillfully described in a few brushstrokes of thick paint.

Wet-in-wet

When a new color is applied over a still-wet one, the two will partially mix. This technique is used in both oil and watercolor painting but is trickier in acrylic.

In oil painting, the method was much used by the Impressionists, notably Claude Monet, who painted landscapes on the spot at great speed. Thick acrylics can be used in the same way, but you will need to mix the colors with a retarding medium.

Watercolor wet-in-wet effects can be achieved, as in watercolor itself, by working on damped paper. As long as the paper stays damp, so will the paint. So, if it begins to dry before you have completed an area, simply spray it over with a plant spray. These are useful in acrylic work as you can keep the paints wet on your palette by occasional spraying.

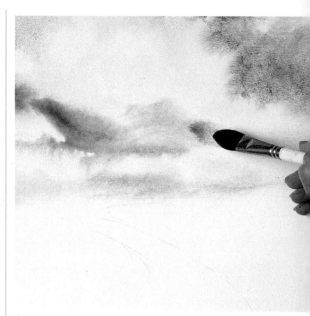

1 Working on well-dampened watercolor paper and using the paint in "watercolor mode," the artist drops one color onto another. As she works, she changes the angle of the board to inhibit or encourage the flow of the paint.

2 Before laying washes for the ground area, the paper was dried with a hairdryer to prevent the colors for land and sky merging. It was then dampened again and further wet-in-wet painting carried out in the area of the foreground.

3 The wet paint is now rubbed with a finger to create smeared lines. As long as the paper remains wet, the paint can be manipulated in a variety of ways. The hairdryer is kept on hand for when it is necessary to arrest the paint flow.

4 Some further work was done on the foreground, and then selected parts of the sky were dampened again to allow the colors of the clouds to be strengthened. Notice the granular effect particularly obvious in the sky. Acrylic used with water alone is prone to "break up" in this way, though the effect also occurs with some watercolor pigments, and is often encouraged by watercolorists.

Combining methods

In *Well Street Common*, Jane Strother worked the foreground and the snow-clad rooftops wet-in-wet, with retarding medium added to medium-thick paint. She also chose a textured paper to allow her also to exploit the dry-brush technique for the tree branches. Notice how the grain of the paper breaks up the brushmarks to give a light, delicate effect.

Colored grounds

Canvasses and boards sold for acrylic painting are usually white, but if you find a white surface distracting you may find it helpful to lay on a tint before starting to paint. There are no true whites in nature, so a white surface provides an artificial standard, making it hard to assess the first colors and tones you put on. There is a tendency to make the first color too light, as almost any color looks dark against white, but if you tint the board with a mid-tone, you can work up to the lightest tones and all the way down to the darks.

Coloring the ground is easily done—brush some thinned acrylic all over the surface and it will be dry in minutes. Usually a neutral color is chosen, such as gray, gray-blue or an ocher brown, which can contrast with the overall color key of the painting. Artists who work on colored grounds often deliberately leave small patches of the ground uncovered, which helps to give the picture unity, as repeating colors from one area to another "ties" the separate elements together.

1 The most usual choice for a colored ground is a neutral brown or gray, but for this vivid subject the artist has decided on a striking multi-colored ground, which she applies with a large soft brush.

2 The undercolors make it easier to be bold about the darkest tones, and here pure black is used.

3 The light and bright colors can also be more easily assessed when there is a ground color, as this provides a middle tone. The reflections have been painted before the black area in front of the fruit; you will see the reason for this in the next step.

4 The black paint is now applied more thinly, in the form of a transparent glaze which will "knock back" the colors of the reflections without obliterating them. The thin paint also allows some of the ground color to show through.

5 Final touches add a little more color to the reflections and paint the cut side of the lemon. Notice the way the ground color has influenced the applied colors, with the black glazes over the blues and violets, producing a deep rich purple, particularly noticeable at the top of the picture.

Tonal underpainting

Before the Impressionists revolutionized oil-painting techniques by working outdoors direct from the subject, paintings were built up in layers, starting with a tonal underpainting—usually brown—which then established the whole composition and all the modeling of forms. Color was applied in the final stages.

Fast-drying acrylic is ideal for such techniques, and some painters have revived traditional oil techniques by building up a whole picture in thin layers of glazing over an underpainting. The method is only suited to studio work, but for any large or complex composition, such as a figure group or highly organized still life, it can be more useful than underdrawing, because it allows you to work out the main light and dark areas.

1 For a painting which is to have a strong tonal structure, an underpainting in black, white and gray can be very successful. The artist begins with a brush drawing.

2 The figure is built up in light gray overlaid with thicker applications of white, which will allow for glazes of light and bright color.

3 The heavy brushstrokes of white show through the transparent red glaze to model the forms. There is little point in making an underpainting unless it plays a part in the finished image.

4 The top colors have been applied thinly everywhere; the modeling on the legs was also achieved by letting the thick, white underpainting show through the watery, blue-gray paint.

Knife painting

Paint applied with a brush can be thin, thick or somewhere in between. However, paint applied with a knife must always be thick.

Knife painting is a form of impasto, but the effect is quite different from that of thick paint applied with a brush. The knife presses the paint onto the surface, giving a flat plane bordered by a ridge where the stoke ends. In a painting built up entirely of knife strokes, these planes and edges will catch the light in different ways, creating a "busy" and interesting picture surface. The marks can be varied by the direction of the stroke and the amount of paint, and you do not have to restrict yourself to the flat of the knife—you can flick paint on with the side to create fine, quite precise lines. As with any impasto method, you will probably need to mix the paint with a bulking medium (see page 20), or it will not be thick enough to hold the marks of the knife.

1 A less-experienced artist might need to make an underdrawing to act as a guide for the first knife strokes, but here, the main shape is blocked in with color immediately. The artist is working on canvas board.

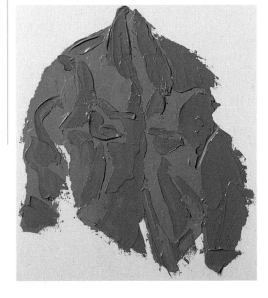

2 The first layer of paint was allowed to become touch dry and a second layer was added with a pointed knife. The first application of paint was pushed onto the surface, so it is relatively flat. The brown has been applied more lightly, creating thick ridges with distinct edges.

3 By twisting the knife slightly as he works, the artist allows the point to scratch into the paint, thus combining knife painting with a version of the sgraffito technique (see page 106).

4 An ordinary, straight-bladed palette knife is now used to remove small areas of the still-wet brown paint, suggesting the buttons on the jacket. Thickly applied paint dries slowly and can be manipulated on the surface for a considerable time.

5 Further knife strokes of both black and white paint were added in the final stages to complete the definition of the jacket.

Extruded paint

As well as being applied with knives and other implements, paint can be squeezed onto the working surface from a nozzle. This method is similar to that used by potters, who create raised patterns by squeezing thinned clay, called slip, onto the surface of plates or bowls. It is also, of course, used by cooks for decorating cakes.

You could squeeze the paint straight from the tube, but this will make rather a thick, unsubtle line, so it is best to fit the tube with a nozzle such as the ones used for cake icing. In this way you can draw directly onto the surface. Or, you can put the paint into an icing bag, either as it is or thickened with an impasto medium—a practical measure as otherwise you will use a lot of paint.

1 A design—based on a high-heeled boot— was worked out in a sketchbook, and guidelines were penciled on the working surface (a canvas board). The artist now begins to build up the picture with varying consistencies of paint.

2 By carrying out several stages of painting, the artist gives himself a foundation on which to begin the extruding. This needs a decisive approach, since mistakes can't easily be corrected.

3 Using a piping bag improvised from tracing paper, he begins to outline the toe of the boot with black. He has bulked out the paint by mixing it with impasto medium.

4 Several piping bags are needed for different colors. A new one is now used to draw rows of carefully spaced diagonal lines around the painted ovals.

Continued on next page

5 The surface is then piped with a network of lines, circles and small dots. Care must be taken not to rest the hand on completed parts of the work, so the board is turned around from time to time.

6 At this stage, the picture is propped up at a distance to assess how much more work needs to be done. The boot clearly requires further attention, as it is less heavily textured than the background.

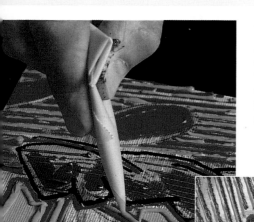

7 The nozzle of the piping bag has been cut to give a thicker trail of paint, and solid orange lines are made inside the earlier red ones.

8 The same orange was used first to outline the boot and then to strengthen the oval shapes in the background. The rest of the boot was built up with a finer network of lines overlaying the original flatly painted colors.

Stenciling

Stenciling is a masking technique in which paint is applied to certain areas of the image while being barred from others. At its simplest, it involves no more than cutting a shape out of a piece of thin card, acetate film or waxed stencil paper, placing this sheet on the working surface, and pushing paint through the "hole." The method is often used for applying decorations to pieces of furniture or walls, and it has interesting possibilities for painting, particularly for any work that emphasizes a flat pattern or the combination of a flat pattern and texture.

The stencil should be relatively simple—a stylized flower or leaf, for example, or one or two geometric shapes. You can repeat the stenciled shape as often as you like, perhaps varying the direction.

1 A shape was cut from waxed stencil paper, and color is pushed onto the paper with a stencil brush. The stencil paper is held firmly with one hand to prevent it slipping.

2 A new stencil has been cut and a band of yellow laid over the blue. The stencil is now turned around, and a further band of iridescent gold laid down. This only partially covers the other colors, because of its transparency.

3 A third stencil, used first in one direction and then the other, gives two fine lines of red. This color is opaque, and will cover the blue more strongly than either the yellow or the gold.

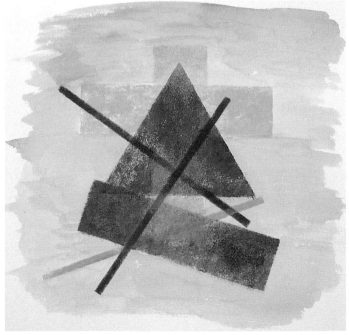

4 One further line of yellow was added to balance the reds, and a light wash was laid over the background. The stencil brush produces a pleasing texture, and the pressure can be varied to create different effects, from solid applications to thin veils of color.

Sgraffito

Sgraffito means scoring into the paint to reveal either the white of the canvas or board or another color below. This is another technique borrowed from oil painting. It is slightly trickier with acrylics because they dry faster, and the paint must remain wet long enough for the scratched pattern to be made. However, if you use reasonably thick paint, or mix it with retarding medium, you should have no problems.

You can make a variety of lines, depending on the implement you use and the consistency of the paint. If you scratch into a fairly thin top layer which has been allowed to dry slightly, using a sharp implement such as a scalpel or the tip of a triangular painting knife, the lines will be fine and crisp. Scoring into thick, wet paint with a blunter implement will yield less precise lines, with ridges of paint on each side of them. This can be effective for detail and texture; for example, you might use the method to describe the bark of a tree, hair, or the pattern of bricks on a wall.

1 Paint can be scratched into to reveal the white surface, but in this case the artist intends to scratch back to another color. She therefore lays a red ground all over the canvas board before painting the fruit and basket.

2 When painting the blue background, she deliberately leaves a little of the red showing between brushstrokes. She will reinforce this color contrast by scratching into the blue later.

3 She has used retarding medium so the paint is still wet enough to be removed with the point of a knife. If it becomes too dry, harder pressure has to be applied, and this can remove the first layer of paint as well as the second.

4 Both the point and the serrated edge of the knife are used to create a variety of lines in the blue background. These are echoed by the small areas of red left uncovered by the blue in the first stages of the painting.

Continued on next page

5 With the fruit now painted, the point of the knife was used to pick out dots of red on the lemon. A light glaze was laid to create the shadow on the left side of the basket, and now the pattern is built up with further knife scratching.

6 To echo the reds elsewhere in the painting and create foreground interest, the tablecloth is also scratched into with the knife.

7 The effect of the painting relies to a large extent on the color scheme which has been well chosen to provide blue/red contrasts in each area. The red sgraffito into blue balances the bright colors of the fruit as well as giving extra impact to the scratched lines.

Scraping

Paint can be squeezed onto the surface, applied with the fingers, put on with a painting knife, and it can also be scraped onto the surface.

This latter method—which can be carried out with an improvised scraper such as a plastic ruler or half an old credit card, or with one of the metal-bladed tools used for removing wallpaper—is allied to knife painting, but produces flatter layers of paint which cover the surface more thinly. It is thus ideal for layering techniques in which transparent paint is scraped over opaque layers or vice versa. You can also scrape lightly tinted acrylic medium over existing color, producing a glazing effect that enriches the color and gives it depth.

1 A plastic card is used to drag paint thinly across the surface. A metal paint scraper can also be used, but the flexibility of plastic makes it more sensitive. The working surface is a canvas board laid flat on a table and secured with tape.

2 A darker color is laid over the blue. Although the paint is at tube consistency, coverage is thin enough to reveal the color beneath, and give an effect almost like that of glazing.

3 The greater rigidity of a paint scraper produces thicker, more irregular coverage, a method that is applied in this example to build up surface texture in places.

4 Here you can see the effect of the paint scraper (the areas of mountain above the trees at top left) and the transparent overlays of color achieved with the plastic card.

Continued on next page

5 The card is pulled downward to create a veil of color which accurately suggests the reflections. The pigment used in this case is relatively transparent.

6 The foliage on the far bank of the lake is built up more thickly. The paint is the same consistency as before, but instead of being dragged across the surface, it is applied in a series of short, interrupted strokes.

7 The finished painting shows a variety of effects that would be impossible to achieve with any conventional painting tool. Thin veils of color contrast with discreet semi-impastos and lively edge qualities.

Thin and thick contrasts

As has been mentioned earlier, acrylic can be used like watercolor, with the picture built up from a series of thin washes of color. The advantage of acrylic over watercolor is that the former is non-soluble when dry, allowing you to superimpose any number of washes—watercolor, however, remains water-soluble, so you can muddy the colors by applying too many layers. For transparent techniques on paper, the best surface is watercolor paper, but these methods are not restricted to works on paper; lovely effects can be achieved by using transparent overlays of color on canvas. These can be juxtaposed with thicker applications of paint, which creates an interesting spatial effect, as the thicker paint comes forward in space.

The American abstract painter Morris Louis (1912–1962) worked on raw (unprimed) canvas, using thin, transparent washes to build up overlapping shapes in brilliant, translucent colors. Similar techniques can be used for representational work.

1 The primed canvas has been dampened all over with a solution of warm water and liquid detergent, which helps to spread the color and gives a soft-edged effect. Color is spread at the top of the upright canvas and allowed to run down.

2 A further application of color blends with the first and creates more runs and dribbles.

3 The pattern of dribbled color is built up and strengthened with dark purple. A soft brush is used to lift out some of this color, creating bands of light and dark.

4 The canvas is now turned upside down, and color is applied at the top in the same way as before but rather more thickly; in this case, the artist wants the paint to run right down the canvas.

Continued on next page

5 Because the photograph was taken when the paint was still wet, the new colors obscure the original purples and reds, but when the paint dries, it becomes more transparent, as you can see in the finished painting.

6 The canvas is turned again, and a new color is applied and allowed to run. The edge that is at the top at this stage is actually the bottom of the painting.

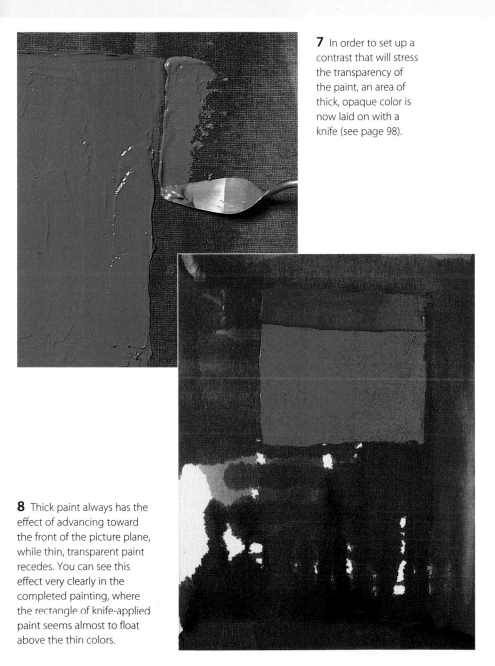

7 In order to set up a contrast that will stress the transparency of the paint, an area of thick, opaque color is now laid on with a knife (see page 98).

8 Thick paint always has the effect of advancing toward the front of the picture plane, while thin, transparent paint recedes. You can see this effect very clearly in the completed painting, where the rectangle of knife-applied paint seems almost to float above the thin colors.

Texturing the surface

Acrylic excels in the area of texture—there is almost nothing you cannot do with it. Textured effects can be created in many different ways, but acrylic modeling paste, which is specially made for underlying textures, is ideal for the dramatic textures shown here. It can be applied to the painting surface in any way you choose, but you must use it on a rigid surface; if applied to canvas, it may crack. You can create rough, random textures by putting the paste on with a palette knife. You can comb it on to make straight or wavy lines, or dab it on with a rag or stiff brush. And you can make regular or scattered patterns by imprinting: spreading the area with modeling paste and pressing objects into it while it is still wet.

The underlying texture method is usually most successful when the paint is applied in thin glazes—opaque paint over texture can look lifeless. However, there are no real rules in painting, and it is up to you to discover what works best.

1 Working on heavy white board, the artist spreads acrylic modeling paste first with a palette knife and now with a steel comb of the type made for texturing plaster.

2 Next, he presses a coin into the surface to make an imprint. Modeling paste will remain wet enough for such methods for some time, if used thickly.

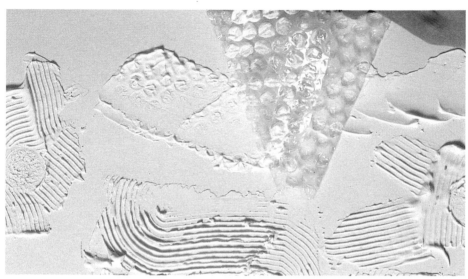

3 Bubble-wrapping also produces an interesting imprint. Each area of texture is kept separate, providing what is in effect a series of individual motifs.

4 When all the motifs have been placed and textured, the whole picture area is sprayed with red liquid acrylic ink (see page 12), using a mouth diffuser. Thinned paint of the same red is now laid in a thick band at the top and allowed to dribble down the surface.

Continued on next page

5 After the paint has begun to settle in and around the troughs of the textured areas, the flow is arrested with a hairdryer.

6 Thicker blue paint is now dragged lightly over the red. Notice that in the more heavily textured areas the color catches only on the ridges.

7 The final stage—and one that has completely transformed the painting—is to spray yellow liquid acrylic over the entire picture surface. In terms of color-mixing, the effect is similar to an overall glaze of color, the yellow mixing with the red and blue to produce orange and a subtle green-blue.

Wax resist

This is a technique that relies on the incompatibility of oil and water. A candle or waxy crayon is used to scribble over clean paper and a wash of water-thinned acrylic is laid on top. The paint slides off the waxed areas, leaving a slightly speckled area of white. You are not limited to white candle or crayon; you can use colored oil pastels, or the newer oil bars, which are excellent for wax resist, making a drawing in several colors which can then be overlaid with a contrasting color of paint.

1 Watercolor paper is tinted with colored gesso, which provides a slight texture as well as reducing the glare of white paper. A pencil drawing is then made as a guide, and wax applied lightly to the top of the cabbage.

2 The thin, watered paint slides off the wax. Thick paint is less suitable for this method, as the tough plastic skin formed by opaque acrylic can cover the wax completely.

3 Further drawing is done with the sharpened end of a household candle. The colored ground helps the artist to see where she is putting the wax; this can be rather a hit-and-miss affair on white paper.

4 Another application of paint builds up the texture, with the paint creating a series of tiny dots, blobs and dribbles as it slips off the wax and settles in the non-waxed areas.

Continued on next page

5 To create more precise, linear effects, the point of a knife is used to scratch away the small drops of paint that have settled on top of the wax. The artist has turned the board around to gain access to this area of the picture.

6 A white oil bar is now used to draw over the paint, giving more definition to the cabbage leaf, which was previously rather amorphous. The bar has also been used to try to reinforce the drawing in the center of the cabbage.

7 Further finishing touches are made with green oil pastel. You can also use oil pastels under the paint, but they are less effective for resist than candle wax or oil bars.

8 The finished picture shows a lively combination of pattern and texture. The oil bar, which has been used on the cabbage and the plate, gives a painterly quality to the image.

Masking

It is extremely difficult to paint a completely clean edge or a perfectly straight line. It can help to hold your brush against a ruler, but the paint tends to slip underneath, so it is better to use masking tape. Masking techniques are often used by abstract painters who want crisp, hard-edged division between shapes, but they have their uses in representational painting also. You might be painting an interior with a window frame, and you could use masking tape to create a sharp division between this and the view outside. Masking tape can be stuck down over thinly applied paint—as long as it is dry—so it can be applied at various stages in a painting.

1 Thin red and yellow paint is streaked onto the surface (canvas board) and allowed to dry before masking tape is applied.

2 The contrast between opaque, flatly applied paint and thinner, rougher applications is to be one of the features of this painting. The brilliant red is applied with a soft brush, which evens out the brushstrokes.

3 The tape is peeled off carefully, leaving a crisp edge. It must be removed before the paint has begun to dry, since the plastic skin that quickly forms will come away with the tape.

4 The red paint has been dried with a hairdryer, more tape applied, and the area between painted in blue before the tape is again removed. It would be virtually impossible to achieve this thin, straight, slightly tapered line by any method other than masking.

Continued on next page

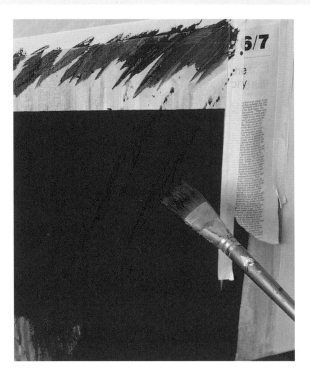

5 To provide a contrast to the flat area of red, thin purple paint is flicked onto the surface and allowed to run down in dribbles. The artist is working with the board upright on an easel to encourage such effects.

6 Because the purple paint was thin it had seeped under the masking tape. The hard edge is reinstated by painting over it first in white and now in yellow.

7 The final stage is a thick application of green over parts of the red, applied with a knife (see page 98).

8 To achieve a contrast of shapes and edge qualities as well as of texture, the final green layer is masked at the top only, and then drawn out to form a series of irregular shapes.

Monoprint

Monoprinting is a cross between printing and painting. In true printmaking, a series of identical or near-identical impressions is taken from the same image, while monoprint, as its name implies, is a "one-off" method. The procedure is simple, and no special equipment is required. A painting—which should be fairly simple and bold—is made on a piece of glass or some other non-absorbent surface. Paper is then laid on top, gently rubbed with your hand, a roller or a spoon, and lifted off. Most of the paint will have been transferred from the original surface to the paper, making the print.

Monoprinting can be done with almost any of the painting media, but when using acrylic you will need to add retarding medium. If the paint has begun to dry before you put the paper on, it will obviously not make a satisfactory print. You will also need to experiment to find the right consistency of paint; it needs to be fairly thick and juicy, but not so thick that it smudges when you press down the paper.

Single-stage print

1 Working rapidly to prevent the colors from drying out before the printing stage, the artist paints the image on a piece of heavy glass. Each area of color is kept separate.

2 Drawing paper is then laid over the painting and rubbed with a spoon to transfer the color to the paper. The pressure can be varied to create different effects.

3 The paper is now lifted carefully away from the glass. At this stage, it can be replaced and rubbed again if it has not absorbed enough color, or it can be dampened to encourage the paint to spread.

4 However fast you work, you will find that some of the paint has begun to dry and will print incompletely. However, this can produce interesting results; you can see this "dry-line" effect on the stems of the plant. The variations in the area of red at the bottom are produced by scribbling on the back of the paper with the handle of the spoon at the printing stage.

Continued on next page

Three-stage print

2 The first painting stage, which will establish the base colors for the print, is now complete.

1 This print is to be more elaborate, with each printing registered (aligned), so a drawing is first made and placed beneath the glass to act as a guide.

3 A print is taken by placing the paper over the glass and rubbing with a spoon. The paper is precisely aligned to the lower left corner of the glass, thus ensuring a correct register for the later printing stages.

4 With the pencil drawing left in exactly the same position as before, a brush drawing is made on the glass, outlining the shapes of the leaves and stems.

5 A print is then made with the paper again carefully aligned to the corner of the glass.

6 For the third printing, which will define the shadows, Payne's gray paint is used alone. Once again, a print is taken over the earlier stages.

7 After the third printing, the image has more depth and definition, while retaining a pleasing softness. Payne's gray is a relatively transparent pigment and has strengthened the earlier colors without obliterating them completely.

Line and wash

Because acrylic can imitate both oil and watercolor, many oil-painting and watercolor techniques can be adapted to the new medium. Line and wash, a traditional watercolor technique, is one example.

The paint for the washes should be kept thin, or it may detract from the effect of the drawing, so it is best to choose the more transparent pigments. The paint can be thinned with water alone, or with a mixture of water and medium.

The kind of pen you choose will depend on the effect you want. Some line and wash drawings are fragile (the technique is much used for flower studies) while others are bold. Experiment with different pens, from fine nibs to fiber- and felt-tipped pens, or even ballpoints—an underrated drawing implement. You might also try using water-soluble ink, which will spread when wet color is laid on top, creating soft, diffused effects.

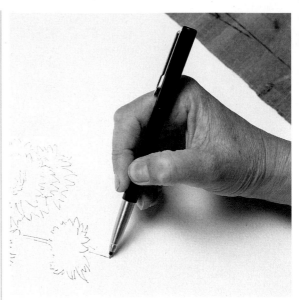

1 Using a fine-pointed reservoir pen, and working on smooth cartridge paper, the artist has drawn in the shapes of the flowers with water-soluble ink.

2 With the paint thinned to watercolor consistency, she now touches in color with a Chinese brush. Because the ink is water soluble, the wet paint spreads it slightly, giving a soft effect.

4 The pen is now used in a more positive way to draw into the leaves with diagonal strokes of hatching and cross-hatching.

3 Further details are added with pen, and green washes are laid on the leaves. These mix with the blue ink to create an impression of light shading on the leaves.

6 To provide a context for the flowers as well as some color contrast, the background wash is extended, and the top of the vase sketched in lightly with a pen.

5 A light wash is laid over the background and taken carefully around the edges of the flowers.

Pastel and acrylic

Almost any drawing medium can be combined with acrylic, and can either exploit the differences between the media or unite them into a homogeneous whole. An example of the latter approach is the technique employed by some pastel artists of making an acrylic underpainting. Sometimes, the whole of this is worked over in pastel, and sometimes parts are left as they are.

Sharper media contrasts can be achieved by starting with acrylic thinned to a watercolor consistency and drawing on top with pastel or oil pastel.

The two media can also be used hand-in-hand. Both acrylic paint and acrylic mediums are excellent fixatives for pastel, so you can build up a painting by a layering method: applying some paint and pastel, then covering the pastel with medium or paint and laying on more. Wet paint or medium can cause the pastel color to spread slightly, but this gives a watercolor effect at the edge of each stroke which can be very attractive.

1 The composition is sketched out in soft pastel, using a combination of linear and side strokes— those made with the side of a short length of pastel.

2 A transparent wash of water-thinned paint is brushed lightly over the pastel. Because the paint forms a plastic skin, it fixes the pastel, allowing you to work on top with no risk of smudging.

3 Further washes are now laid over the background area. The artist develops the two media together, so that the painting has a unity of technique from the outset.

4 At this stage, the effect is similar to that given by the line and wash method (see page 134), with paint of a watercolor consistency laid over the pastel marks.

Continued on next page

5 The artist continues to build up the painting with both paint and pastel. Because the watercolor paper has a slightly rough surface, it breaks up the pastel marks to provide a broken-color effect.

6 In the foreground, linear strokes made with the edge of a nylon brush complement the previously made pastel marks.

7 The side of the pastel stick is dragged lightly over dry paint, creating a subtle veil of color. This area of the painting—the middle distance—requires a softer treatment than the foreground.

8 The finished painting is a good example of a successful "marriage" of media. Although there is a contrast of textures, no one area can be singled out as being either paint or pastel.

Charcoal and acrylic

Since acrylic paints can be used thinly on paper, very much like watercolor or gouache paint, it follows that you can combine them with any drawing medium that you would use on paper.

Charcoal is, in itself, a versatile medium, capable of producing both fine lines and rich areas of tone. By combining it with acrylic, you can achieve a wide range of exciting effects.

There are many different ways of working. For a portrait you might map out the composition with charcoal, using it also to block in the background, then paint the face and head before working into this with more charcoal. For a landscape you might begin with loose overall washes of color, and then use charcoal to define detail and build up areas of darker tone.

1 The artist has begun with loose washes of color, keeping the paint fairly thin, and now uses a stick of thick charcoal to draw over and into the paint.

2 The paint is built up more thickly, laid around and between the charcoal lines on the patterned fabric. While still wet, the whole of the left side of the picture is sprayed with water, using a mouth diffuser.

3 In this detail, you can see the effect of the water spray which has created a soft, granular texture. The paper is allowed to dry before the artist continues working into the paint with the charcoal.

4 The charcoal drawing on the fabric is now complete, and a small bristle brush is used to dab in touches of magenta. This brilliant color provides a balance for the hot color of the suitcase, which might otherwise have been seen as too dominant.

5 Finishing touches are the addition of highlights on the metal fitting of the suitcase and some further charcoal drawing on the table.

Oil and acrylic

Mixtures of oil and acrylic must be handled with care, as oil and water are incompatible. This does not matter if the oil color is used over the water-based acrylic, but if water-based paint is applied on top of oil, cracking will occur. This might not be immediately apparent; if you use the acrylic thickly it could seem to be going on normally, but it would be unlikely to stand the test of time.

However, acrylic can be used quite safely for the first stages of a work to be completed in oil. This can save a good deal of time for any picture to be built up in layers over an underpainting, as the first applications of color will dry much faster than oils.

You can also cover any kind of acrylic texturing with oil paint, or contrast areas of acrylic with areas of oil. Such methods could be used in collage work, where a lively picture surface produced by contrasting textures is often a feature.

1 Broad areas of tone and color can be established very quickly with an acrylic underpainting. The paint has been applied flatly for the background, as the textures are to be built up with thicker brushstrokes of oil paint.

2 The artist has now begun to apply oil paint over the acrylic. The sunflower was not underpainted, but reserved as white canvas in order to increase the brilliance of the yellows.

ARTIST'S TIP

Unless you want to make a feature of texture it is best to keep the acrylic underpainting fairly thin or it may be difficult to cover with the oil paint. It is normally best used to establish tones or color. However, a textured layer of acrylic could be a basis for thin glazes of oil.

Pencil and acrylic

Pencil can be used under washes of acrylic color or on top of paint that is transparent or opaque. If you are using transparent techniques, one of the problems inherent in acrylics can be used to advantage. For watercolors and for watercolor effects in acrylic, you need a good underdrawing. In actual watercolor work, this can be erased after the first washes are in place, but this is not possible with acrylic, which acts as a fixative on the drawing. So try making the drawing a part of the picture from the start, laying colors over and around pencil lines and adding pencil as the picture takes shape.

Opaque paint will, of course, obscure your original drawing, but you can still use pencil on top. How much you use and in what way depends on the effect you want to achieve: you might reserve the pencil drawing for small areas of detail or pattern, or for parts of the picture which are easier to draw than to paint, such as flowers, stems, the edges of leaves, or facial features.

1 The shape of the building is blocked in with thin paint, and the artist begins to draw into it as soon as it is dry, using a graphite stick—a pencil without the usual wooden casing.

2 Having applied a loose blue wash for the sky, she now starts defining the details at the top of the tower. Graphite (or pencil) is excellent for this, and much quicker than working with paint and a small brush.

3 The shapes of the palm leaves have been built up with a mix of brushstrokes and graphite drawing. Now a small brush is used to pick out some highlights with pale blue-gray paint.

4 The rough stonework (on the left of this photograph) and the graphite stick come into play again for the shadow below the small outgrowths of shrubbery.

5 In the final stages, more graphite drawing is done on the building, giving an accurate impression of the textures of the old plaster and stonework. The drawing, the light colors, and the free brushwork in the sky all contribute to the atmosphere.

Watercolor and acrylic

Watercolor painters often use a touch of "body color" (opaque paint) here and there, perhaps to sharpen a foreground, to add white highlights, or simply to correct a mistake. Usually, gouache paint is used, but acrylic is a better choice, as it does not give such a flat, dead surface.

Paintings that are officially classified as watercolor in exhibition catalogs frequently include acrylic, and if the acrylic is used skillfully, it is often impossible to tell which is which. The trick is to reserve the pure watercolor for any areas that need its particular translucent quality, and to use the acrylic fairly thinly—it should be capable of covering colors below, but should not stand out from the surface. In a landscape with grass and trees in the foreground, for example, you would use pure watercolor for the sky and the far distance, and acrylic, either on its own or over watercolor washes—for the foreground and perhaps any areas of texture in the middle distance, such as a wall or group of houses.

Combining media

Hazel Harrison's *View Over Ullswater* was planned and begun as watercolor and had reached an advanced stage before it became apparent that things were going wrong, particularly with the foreground and the tree on the right. Rather than abandon it, the artist decided to carry out a rescue operation with acrylic, thinned with both water and matt medium to reduce its opacity.

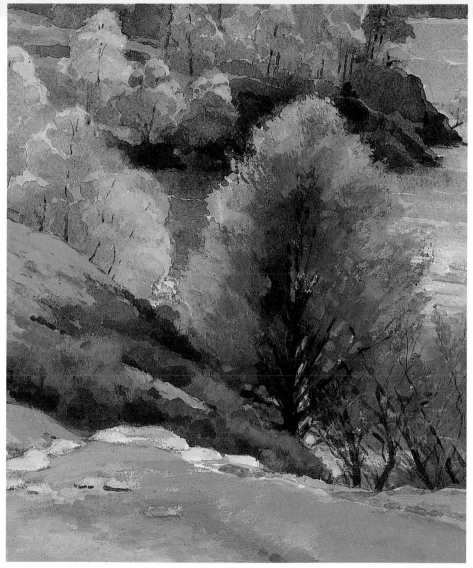

Acrylic was used only for the problem areas of foreground and tree, both of which lacked definition. The effect is very similar to that of watercolor thickened with white gouache, but the artist is accustomed to working in acrylic and finds it easier to handle.

Collage

The word collage comes from the French *coller*, to stick, and it describes a picture made by gluing pieces of colored paper, fabric, photographs, newspaper clippings—or anything you like—onto a working surface. These can be combined with paint, or the whole composition can consist of glued-on fragments.

Acrylic is the perfect medium for collage work. Both paints and mediums have powerful adhesive properties and are capable of securing quite heavy objects to the picture surface. If you use the texture paste (see pages 20 and 118) and press objects into it—these might be shells, scraps of tree bark, grasses, or even beads or small pieces of jewelry—you can create three-dimensional effects akin to relief sculpture.

Alternatively, you can use paint and paper alone, placing the emphasis on two-dimensional pattern and the juxtaposition of colors. Some artists employ a layering technique, gluing on fragments of colored paper with acrylic medium, covering these with paint and medium, then repeating the process. Others will begin painting and then collage certain areas.

Mixed-media approaches

Although Mike Bernard's painting on paper, *View of Mousehole*, contains elements of collage, the artist prefers to describe it as a mixed media painting, because he does not rely on collage alone to produce areas of texture. He has combined collage with pastel, paint and colored inks, applied with a number of different tools, such as rollers, sponges, toothbrushes, and palette knives.

Tissue-paper collage

Jill Confavreux's painting *Winter Lake* evolved as part of a series on the theme of frozen ground. The working surface was a medium watercolor paper, onto which the artist glued acid-free tissue paper with gloss medium. This texture formed a textured "ground" over which she painted and poured acrylic glazes, followed by a light scumble of gold and silver oil pastels. These acted as a resist (see page 122) for further applications of paint, creating an exciting and unusual range of effects.

Surface texture

Jacquie Turner has used collage in certain areas of *Chiswick House Grounds* to create additional texture, which is always an important element in her work. Pieces of glued-on tissue paper are combined with acrylic paint and colored inks, watercolor, gouache and pastel.

4
Subjects

Landscape **Trees**

Trees can be some of the most exciting features of landscapes, inviting a number of treatments. Tall trees in the foreground of a landscape, for instance, allow you to introduce a pattern element, contrasting verticals and horizontals; while massed trees in the middle distance create satisfying tall or bulky shapes, and often an array of contrasting colors.

Trees can also be appreciated for their varying textural qualities and painted from a close viewpoint—tree barks, for example, provide a wealth of fascinating detail as well as rich variations in color.

Framing a view

The focal point in Gerry Baptist's *Italian Trees* is the distant hills, and the artist has employed a classic compositional device to emphasize it: using the dark foreground trees as a frame within a frame. This also increases the sense of space, as the cropping of the trees at the top brings them to the front of the picture, pushing the hills back.

Soft effects

Colored and textured mountboard without priming was used for Alan Oliver's *Glandsford Church*. The artist likes a slightly absorbent surface, which allows him to exploit dry-brush techniques: notice how the paint has been dragged lightly over the surface to achieve the soft effect of the trees. Apart from the sky, which is a thin wash of color, the paint has been used straight from the tube with no water or medium added.

Continued on next page

First-hand observation

Paul Powis does not restrict his outdoor work to the summer months, and these evergreen trees were painted on the spot during winter. There is a strong pattern element in *West Malvern Spring*, with an exciting interplay of diagonals and verticals offset by intricately shaped areas of bright and dark color. The clumps of foliage have been defined by painting the sky around them last, light over dark.

Creating impressions

Although there has been no attempt to describe the trees in detail, they are completely convincing in Geoff Pimlott's *Hillside Fields*, with the impression of the foliage built up through directional brushstrokes. The painting, on primed canvas, was worked in the studio from sketchbook drawings.

Descriptive paint

The tree trunk in Ted Gould's *Spring*, which forms a dramatic foreground to this painting on canvas, has been beautifully observed and described—notice the variety of colors in this one area, and the fine marks made with a small brush to suggest the texture. The foliage of the left-hand tree has been painted with small strokes of impasto over thinner paint.

Landscape **Hills and mountains**

In flat landscapes, the sky often plays a major role in the composition; indeed this pre-eminence of sky is part of their appeal. Hills and mountains, however, will always dominate a composition, with the sky playing a minor part, if any. The shapes they create are a gift to the artist, from the gentle curves of downland to the jagged formations seen in cliffs or high mountain ranges.

Fast-drying acrylics are ideal for crisp, positive effects, allowing you to exploit edge qualities to the full, either with successive, overlaid, thin washes or thicker applications of paint laid on with a brush or knife, and left unblended. For the softer effects of hills, try letting your brush follow the direction of the curves, both to build up the forms and to create a feeling of movement.

Color unity

Judy Martin's large painting on paper, *Downs View 1* was done in the studio from sketches, which allowed for a more personal and interpretative use of color than is usually possible when working on the spot. It can be difficult to paint a sky yellow, for example, when faced with the blue or gray reality, but in this case it was the right choice, as it echoes the foreground yellow to unify sky and land without in any way interfering with our perception of the landscape.

Stress a focal point

Working on watercolor paper, Helena Greene has concentrated on the pattern of angular shapes made by the play of light on the mountains. The deep purple-blue of the sky forms a dramatic backdrop, and the dark shape in the center of the road echoes those of the mountains, providing a lead-in to the focal point of *The Karakorum Highway*.

Exploring color

Jill Confavreux's *Himalyan Poppyscape*, in acrylic and collage with oil pastel, evolved from the idea of exploring the color blue through many different textures of paint and paper. Working on watercolor board, the artist began with a series of acrylic glazes, encouraging the colors to run and mingle. The paper for collaging— Japanese Hokai paper and tissue paper—was then painted in turn before being stuck down with gloss medium, left to dry, and scumbled over with oil pastel. The artist then added more acrylic glazes, and cut back into the board in places to create a different surface for further applications of paint and oil pastel.

Landscape **Water**

Perhaps because of its unique qualities of being both a transparent substance and a mirror, water has always fascinated artists—lakes, rivers and seas are among the most popular of all landscape subjects. A still lake, gleaming pale blue or silver-white in the reflected light from the sky—even if it is only glimpsed in the distance—can provide a center of interest for a landscape painting, while reflections, or the patterns made by moving water, can form the main subject.

Creating movement

The choppy water and the movement of the boats in *Sigmas Racing* are conveyed through inventive and varied brushwork, finger smudging and scraping. Jacquie Turner likes to work on smooth paper so that she can move the paint around, and she combines standard acrylic with "liquid acrylic" inks, watercolor and touches of collage.

Mixing media

In *Lily Pads: Frog Pond in October*, Simie Maryles has used a combination of acrylic and pastel, working on heavy illustration board. Many different colors have been used for the water, and the deep, brilliant blue in the immediate foreground helps to bring this area of the painting forward.

Simplification

The brilliant blue of the water combined with the contrasting red-brown reflections in Ted Gould's *Autumn Scene* form the center of interest in this attractive painting on canvas board. The paint has been used thickly, mixed with a retarding medium, and the colors have been simplified into bold blocks for maximum impact.

Continued on next page

Foregrounds

In this on-the-spot sketchbook study, Gerry Baptist has made the bold decision to leave the foreground blank, save for a hint of yellow reflected from the sky and a small patch of darker ripples on the left—which brings the area into focus. There is just enough movement on the water surface to blur the reflections of the trees, which are treated with horizontal brush-marks, in contrast to the more energetic marks used for the trees themselves.

Descriptive marks

Lively, active marks are used throughout Jacquie
Turner's *Along the Thames from Under Richmond
Bridge 1*, integrating the water and reflections with
the boats and trees. The artist has combined acrylic
in both pot and tube form with a number of other
media, including watercolor, chalk, wax crayon and
fabric paint, and has worked on smooth-surfaced
watercolor paper.

Tutorial **Acrylic and oil pastel**

A marriage of acrylic and soft oil pastel is skillfully exploited in this lovely evocation of a woodland landscape by Debra Manifold. It has been done from a photographic reference, but with a considerable input of memory and experience.

1 A ground of tinted acrylic gesso is laid on white canvas board to "cut" the white and provide a light texture, always important for work involving the use of pastels.

2 Working initially in only two colors, the artist establishes the "skeleton" of the composition and sets a key for the color scheme. The yellow and purple, although they will be modified later, will both play an important part in the finished painting.

3 An irregular horizontal band of white has been scumbled lightly across the painting over the original colors, and transparent blues and greens are now applied on top, using bold directional brushstrokes.

4 The brush is drawn lightly down the canvas in a dry-brush method to achieve a delicate broken-color effect. This thin coverage of paint also facilitates the later application of pastel.

Continued on next page

5 Strokes of white pastel are now applied, taking care that the marks of the pastel stick complement the earlier brushstrokes. The very soft oil pastel creates a painterly rather than a linear effect.

6 Transparent paint has been laid over the pastel in places, and now more pastel is applied, gradually building up the effect of dappled light by means of a layering technique.

7 This detail shows the effect of the layering method. The oil pastel acts as a resist for thin paint applied on top; you can see this in the area on the left, where the green pastel is visible through the indigo paint.

Debra Manifold
Sunlight Through Trees
The combination of transparent acrylic glazes and oil pastel has achieved a wonderful depth of color, and the lively brush and pastel work give a sense of movement, evoking the ephemeral qualities of ever-changing light and shadow.

Buildings **Urban scenes**

All towns and cities have their own particular feeling, so if you are painting townscape rather than "portraits" of individual buildings, try to analyze what this feeling is, and find ways of creating a sense of place by giving visual clues. In an exotic location, for example, people's clothing and characteristic postures will be strong indicators; while in a busy modern city, you can make cars and typical "street furniture" part of the composition.

It is often possible to convey a sense of place through color or texture alone, making a play of light, bright colors or strong tonal contrasts in a sunny Mediterranean town, and exploiting "low-key" colors, such as grays and browns, in a northern industrial setting. Or, you could make a feature of rough stone or peeling plaster on old buildings, or the smooth or reflective surfaces of new ones.

Photographic realism

In Brian Yale's painting of London's Monument and the surrounding buildings, the approach is almost photographic, with minute attention paid to every detail and texture. The composition is beautifully worked out, with the diagonal line formed by the edge of the dark shadow leading the eye up the right-hand building and the crane that forms a balance for the Monument.

Landscape features

Gary Jeffrey's lovely painting *Ipswich Docks* shows urban landscape at its most appealing—a true marriage of man-made and natural features. The artist has worked on canvas and his painting technique is similar to an oil-painter's, with the paint built up from thin to thick, and some use of wet-into-wet techniques, particularly in the reflections.

Modern buildings

One of the most exciting visual phenomena in modern cities is that of reflections in the many large expanses of glass, often distorted in intriguing ways. In *The New City*, Richard French has mimicked the effect of such reflections by using multiple layers of acrylic glazes, working on a smooth-surfaced acid-free mount-board known as museum board. The painting is a large one, and to facilitate handling it was painted in three separate sections.

continued on next page

Atmosphere

Neil Watson's *Broad Street, Oxford* is full of atmosphere and movement, the latter quality emphasized by the energetic brushwork. The paint has been used thinly—notice how it has dribbled down the board in the sky area—and some linear detail has been added with inks.

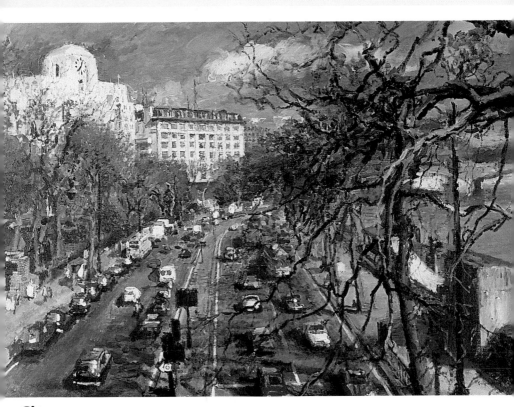

Cityscapes

Cityscapes are often avoided by amateur painters, but they can be a
very rewarding subject, as Gary Jeffrey's *Spring on the Embankment*
shows. He has chosen a high viewpoint, presumably from a window,
which has allowed him to treat the cars as vivid patches of color
contrasting with the white slabs of the buildings.

Buildings **Individual buildings**

It is sometimes the hustle and bustle of a townscape that provides the stimulus for a painting, but some buildings invite a close, more portrait-like approach, either because they are beautiful in themselves or because they possess some striking quality of shape or texture.

If shape is the important element, you will obviously want to show the whole of the building, but texture, which can be one of the most attractive and painterly aspects of architectural subjects, can often be treated by taking a closer view and "cropping in" so that these surface qualities become virtually the subject of the painting.

Collage

This is a technique particularly well-suited to architectural subjects, and in Mike Bernard's *Backs of Buildings, St Mary's Road, Southampton*, cut and glued paper has been used in conjunction with acrylic, inks and pastel. The varieties of paper used for collaging give an impression of textures without attempting to imitate reality. The printed-paper on the right-hand area of the foreground has been placed upside down to prevent it from being over-obtrusive.

Focusing in

In *Woman and Dark Doorway*, Jill Mirza has taken a close view and made the texture of the flaking wall and the interplay of darks and lights the joint subjects of the painting. Working on canvas, she has used the paint both thick and thin, sometimes scumbling very thin colors over much thicker applications.

Painting textures

Texture is the main preoccupation In Nick Harris's *Openings 46— Wooden House*, and it has been portrayed with great skill. Working on watercolor paper, the artist has built up the painting in a layering technique with a succession of thin washes.

Buildings **Interiors**

The possibilities of interiors are often overlooked, but room settings provide a wealth of compositional possibilities, with the shapes of furniture and objects contrasting with the linearity of architectural features, such as doors and windows.

An alternative approach is to paint an interior much as you would a still life, focusing on one part of the room—perhaps a mantelpiece or window. Or you can bring in an element of landscape painting, using part of the room as an "introduction" to a view through the window, as in Daniel Stedman's painting. Light can play a vital part in the composition also. For example, light coming in through a window creates a marvelous interplay of light and dark colors which allows you to introduce a pattern element. Artificial light can also be used to advantage; a lamp casting a soft glow on surrounding objects can be the ideal focal point in an interior painting.

Uniting the picture planes

The "inside-outside" theme requires careful control of tones and colors. Too much contrast in the landscape part of the painting or too little in the foreground will destroy the sense of space. Also, the painting will fail to hang together as a composition if the colors used for the inside element are too different from those of the landscape. In Daniel Stedman's *Winter Morning*, the subject has been handled with confidence— the red-brown of the house is echoed on and below the window frame, and the dark tones of the plant, bars and top of the window bring this area forward.

Abstract values

Roy Sparkes's starkly geometric composition
Corridor to Sound Studio Under Construction is
one of several inspired by a visit to a converted
wharf in Liverpool. The careful arrangement of
shapes, colors and light and dark tones give the
work a strong abstract quality; it can be "read"
both as an arrangement of shapes and colors
and as the representation of an interior.

Painting light

Light is the major theme of
this lovely painting, which is
reminiscent of the works of Pierre
Bonnard, one of the greatest
painters of domestic interiors. In
John Rosser's *Teatime View*, the
view though the window is
unimportant, though the window
bars serve a compositional
function in providing a geometric
anchor for the gentle curves made
by the white-clad figures.

Still life **Shapes and textures**

From a purely learning point of view, still life has many advantages. You can paint whatever you choose, arranging the group as you like to provide an interesting composition and combination of color and shapes. But it is more than just a means of practicing your painting skills; it is also a highly satisfying branch of painting.

If still life is less popular than it should be, this may be simply because the breadth of choice makes it difficult to know where to begin. Floral groups, fruit and vegetables, rich textures and reflective surfaces are frequent choices, and rewarding to paint, but many more commonplace objects can form the basis of a still life. Examples might be a pile of books on a table, a pair of shoes in the corner of a room, kitchen utensils hanging on hooks, or your paintbrushes left in a jar after a working session.

Surface pattern

The cloves of garlic curving from the top to the bottom of the painting in Helena Greene's *String of Garlic* make a lively pattern of light on dark, balanced by the orange-reds of the flowers on the right. The artist has not attempted to describe the objects literally, or to mimic their textures—the painting has its own pattern and surface texture and exists independently of the subject matter.

Fruit textures

Texture plays a major role in Doreen Bartlett's delightfully simple but carefully composed *Fruit Still Life*. The smooth surface of the apple has been achieved by blending methods, overlays of color and transparent washes, while dry brush has been used for the tablecloth and areas of the orange.

Exploring shapes

In Sara Hayward's *Shapes 11*, the artist's interest is in the juxtaposition of shapes, as the title implies, and a child's toy has provided a subject which seems tailor-made for the theme. Notice how the objects have been arranged to form a lively composition, with the triangle of the table top at the bottom of the picture echoing and balancing the smaller triangles and other shapes of the toy.

Still life **Floral groups**

A flower group, however simple, needs care in the initial arrangement and equal care in the composition of the painting. Once you have arranged the flowers, think about how you will place the group on the paper or canvas. You will sometimes find that you have a blank space at either side of the vase, and you may need to introduce some additional element to create interest in the foreground. A frequently used device is to place one of the blooms on the table beside the vase, or to scatter a few petals.

If you are painting tall flowers or a wide-spreading arrangement, you may be able to create a better composition by "cropping," that is, allowing one or two blooms or stems to go out of the picture at the top or sides. This suggests that the group has its own life, continuing beyond the confines of the picture area, whereas showing the whole of an object "freezes" it at a certain point in space.

Color harmonies

Valentina Lamdin's lovely painting on canvas, *Lilac Time*, derives much of its impact from the broad mass of glowing color, though there is also enough detail to enable the viewer to identify the flowers. The colors have been chosen with care to provide both an overall harmony and touches of contrast, and the warm pink and violets have been carried through into the background and foreground to unite each area of the painting.

Creating a broad impression

Jacquie Turner's *Bluebells and other Spring Flowers* has a similar subject matter and arrangement to Valentina Lamdin's, but the treatment could not be more different. Here the artist has taken a more impressionistic approach, expressing the brilliant colors and living quality of the flowers through an inventive use of paint and surface texture. The painting is on smooth watercolor paper, with various media such as wax crayon and chalk used with pot and tube acrylic. There are also touches of collage— small pieces of pre-painted tissue paper stuck on with acrylic medium.

Continued on next page

Unusual formats

The wide, horizontal format chosen for Mike Bernard's collage-and-mixed-media flower group has allowed the artist to make the most of the flowers and stems while reducing the vase to little more than a suggestion of a shape. The background is always an important element in still-life compositions, and in *Poppies* it has been fully integrated into the painting, with the shapes, colors and textures echoing those of the flowers.

Tone and color

Contrasts of tone play an important part in Jeremy Galton's beautifully balanced composition. The near-black background makes the perfect foil for the glowing color of the rose, and the dark leaves and brilliant highlights on the glass standing out against the brown of the table top. *The Red Rose* is a small painting, done on smooth mount-board with a yellow-brown priming.

Cropping

Gerry Baptist has made clever use of the cropping device in *My Mother's Jug*, and the sense of movement is enhanced by the deliberate tilting of the jug, and the broad brushstrokes in the background that follow the direction of the stems.

Tutorial **Using a restricted palette**

A still life of fruit on a metal plate, a glass of wine, and dried flowers in a raffia container provides Ted Gould with a colorful subject and an interesting and challenging contrast of textures. He has used only eight colors for the painting, as he finds that a limited palette makes it easier to achieve a unity of color by restricting the possible permutations for mixtures. His choice of colors is: titanium white, Mars black, deep violet, cobalt blue, naphthol crimson, cadmium yellow light, cadmium yellow and chromium oxide green.

1 The painting surface is a white primed canvas, on which a line drawing was first made in yellow, followed by a thin underpainting in mixtures of crimson and two shades of yellow. The colors, mixed on a paper palette, are sprayed with water to keep them moist.

2 The paint is now made more opaque and slightly thicker by the addition of white, which had not been used previously. At this stage, more colors have been laid out on the palette, but the range is deliberately restricted.

3 The artist works from the back to the front of the painting, viewing it as a series of planes. With the dark and light tones of the background drapery in place, he can more easily assess the strength of color and variations of tone needed in the foreground.

4 As he works, he constantly assesses one patch of color against another. The reds he is using for the flowers, the wine and the nectarine are intentionally similar, as he wants to maintain a unity of color throughout the picture.

Continued on next page

5 Further work is done on the plate with a small brush, paying particular attention to the contrast of tones and colors caused by the reflections in the metal. Notice how many different colors have been used in this area alone.

6 The most important detail is the rim of the glass, previously left unpainted in order to maintain the continuity of the drapery seen through the top of the glass. The rim is now painted very carefully with a small sable brush—ellipses are always tricky.

7 One of the joys of leaving the details until last is that you can save up the pleasure of putting in the highlights and seeing the whole painting come to life.

Ted Gould
Still Life with Fruit
The brushwork is vigorous as well as descriptive, and the painting glows with color. The green of the background and the deep purplish grays of the plate and drapery provide the necessary touches of contrast to offset the predominant reds and oranges.

People **Portraits**

The primary task of a portrait is to produce a likeness of the sitter, but it doesn't end there. A portrait is a painting as well, and, therefore, to succeed in terms of art it must meet the usual criteria of composition, balanced color, and successful rendering of three-dimensional form.

It should also convey something of the character and atmosphere of the person, and a device often used by portrait painters is to show the sitter with a selection of his or her personal possessions. This can take the form of a "mini-still life" of objects, but another approach is to paint people in their own homes rather than asking them to come to yours. The color schemes and furnishings people choose are highly expressive of them, as are the clothes they wear.

Painting children

Children are not the easiest of portrait subjects, but can often be painted in short sessions when absorbed by some favorite activity, as in Ted Gould's charming study, *Girl Reading*. The artist has worked on canvas board, starting with a thin underpainting and building up gradually to thick impasto. He uses retarding medium to enable him to manipulate the paint for a longer period.

Head-and-shoulders portraits

In this portrait on canvas board, *Jean's Father*, Gerry Baptist has used a traditional compositional arrangement for head-and-shoulders portraits, cropping the head on the right and thus allowing more space in the direction of the sitter's gaze. The dark background accentuates the vivid red of the jacket and the bright colors used for the face itself.

Heightened colors

The hands and head at the sides of Gerry Baptist's unusual self-portrait are ambiguous: they may represent an audience—the viewers of the painting process—or they may be pointing out some misdemeanour. They also play a part in the composition, as they focus all our attention on the face, whose rich colors have been achieved by laying both opaque paint and transparent glazes over a brilliant red underpainting.

People **Figures in landscape**

Figures in landscape can be a branch of portraiture, or a figure can be used simply to provide a focal point or to explain the scale. The way you treat the figure or figures obviously depends on which approach you are taking. A distant or middle-ground figure can often be treated quite sketchily, but when the figures are in the foreground, as in both the paintings shown here, you must engage with them in more detail. However, you don't always want them to dominate the painting, so if this is not your intention, you must find ways of integrating them into the landscape.

People don't stay still for long, so you will usually have to work from either photographs or sketches, or a combination of both, but if you are making sketches with a particular painting in mind, make sure that you give some indication of both the direction of the light and the scale of the figures in relation to the landscape, as otherwise you will find it difficult to integrate the two elements of the painting.

Making visual links

Ted Gould has cleverly integrated the figure into the landscape in *Woman with Cat* so that figure and trees form a continuous pattern across the picture surface. The artist appears to be more concerned with the interplay of colors and shapes than with creating space or building form—there is the bare minimum of modeling on the figure. Notice how the repetition of colors ties the figure to the landscape elements. The red of the jacket appears in the foreground flowers and left-hand tree trunk, while the dark blue of the jeans is repeated behind the figure and on the hair.

Dominant figues

In Bart O'Farrell's *Daffodil Pickers*, the figures dominate the landscape, which is treated in detail only where it surrounds and explains the activities of the men—the distant hills are merely suggested by slight tonal variations. The composition is masterly, with the first three figures forming a sharp triangle from which the eye is led along the light line of grass by the fourth tiny, crouched shape. The colors, too, are scrupulously controlled; the yellow of the garments has been "knocked back" so that it does not stand out too strongly against the misty background.

Index

A

acetate film 104
acrylic modeling paste 23
acrylics
    artists' colors 11
    the binder 10
    charcoal and acrylic 140-41
    flow-formula paint 11, 26
    full-bodied paints 11
    and glazing 86
    mixing acrylic and oil 162-5
    oil and acrylic 142-3
    paint pots 11
    painting sets 10
    pastel and acrylic 136-9
    pencil and acrylic 144-5
    and sgraffito 106
    students' colors 10
    and tonal underpainting 96
    tube sizes 11
    water-based 10
    watercolor and acrylic 146-7
    and wax resist 122
acrylics, liquid 12-13
    acrylic inks 12, 12, 119
    chroma color 13, 13
alizarin crimson 48, 50, 51, 52
artists' colors 11

B

ballpoints 114
blending 28, 78-9, 175
    and retarding medium 20
"blending brushes" 80
blotting 82, 83
"body color" (opaque paint) 148
bright green 55
bristle brushes 14, 30, 58, 72,
    78, 80, 82, 90, 141
broken color 28
brush mixing 53
brushes 14-15

"blending" 80
bristle 14, 30, 58, 72, 78,
    80, 82, 90, 141
brush care 15
Chinese 134
hardened 91
nylon 14, 73, 79
soft 73, 80, 86, 94
square-ended 80
stencil 104, 105
bubble-wrapping 119
building up 72-7
    medium consistency paint
        on paper 72-3
    thick paint on paper 74-5
    transparent paint on paper
        76-7
buildings 166-73
    individual buildings 170-71
    interiors 172-3
    urban scenes 166-9
bulking medium 20, 98
burnt sienna 49, 55, 65
burnt umber 50

C

cadmium green 51
cadmium orange 51
cadmium red 48, 50, 52, 54,
    60, 61, 64
cadmium yellow 51, 52, 54,
    58, 60
cadmium yellow deep 48, 57,
    62, 63
cadmium yellow lemon 48, 56,
    60, 61, 62, 63
candle 122, 123, 125
canvas
    home-made canvas boards
        32-3
    stretching 34-5
    thick paint on 74-5

capillary matting 19
cerulean blue 50, 51, 62, 65
chalk 161
charcoal 70
    charcoal and acrylic 140-41
children, painting 184
Chinese brush 134
chroma color 13, 13
chromium oxide green 49
cling film 18, 19
cobalt blue 51, 57, 58, 62, 65
collage 148-9, 157, 158, 177, 178
    individual buildings 170
    mixed-media approaches
        148
    surface texture 149
    tissue-paper collage 149
color wheel 42
    basic 43
    pigment 43
colored grounds 94-5
colors
    a basic palette 48-9
    complementary 24, 43, 44-7
    heightened 185
    knocking back 44, 55, 55,
        95, 187
    laying out and mixing 52-3
    learning 54-5
    lightening and darkening
        50-51
    mixing colorful neutrals 55
    modifying 54
    neutral 54, 55
    overlaying 50, 50
    personal approaches 66-7
    primary 42-3
    secondary 42, 43
    tertiary 42
complementary colors 24,
    43, 55

juxtaposing
   complementaries 44
   mixing neutrals 44
   neutralizing colors 44
   optical mixing 45
   using 46-7
contrasts
   rugged effects 24
   subtle 24
   thin and thick 114-17
cooking parchment 19
crayon, wax 122, 161
cropping 170, 176, 179, 185
cross-hatching 135

D
dark over light 27
deep brilliant red 60, 61, 64
deep violet 56, 57
dioxazine purple 49, 50, 52, 54, 57
direct painting 28
dry brush 78, 80-81, 93, 163, 175
"dry-line" effect 131

E
extruded paint 100-103

F
fabric paint 161
Fauve painters 67
floral groups 176-9
   color harmonies 176
   creating a broad impression 177
   cropping 179
   tone and color 178
   unusual formats 178
flow-formula paint 11, 26
focal point 152, 156
focusing in 171
fork 29

fruit textures 175
full-bodied paints 11

G
gesso 36, 162
glass 72, 75, 77
glazing 10, 14, 27, 86-9
   mixing by glazing 56-7
   using glazes 58, 58, 59
gouache effects 31, 31
gouache paint 146, 147
granulation 27
graphite stick 144, 145
greens, mixing 62-3
grounds, colored 94-5

H
hairdryer 92, 93, 120, 127
hatching 135
heavy gel mediums 20, 20, 22, 22, 28, 91
highlights 26, 31, 59, 72, 73, 75, 141, 145
hills and mountains 156-7
   color unity 156
   exploring color 157
   stress a focal point 156
hues, modifying 55, 55

I
impasto 14, 23, 28, 53, 90-91, 98, 155, 184
   and extruded paint 100, 101
   under glazing 90
   using gel medium 91
   using the paint consistency 91
Impressionists 92, 96
imprinting 118
inks
   acrylic 12, 12, 119
   water-soluble 134

interference colors 23, 24, 24
interiors 172-3
   abstract values 173
   painting light 173
   uniting the picture planes 172
iridescent medium 22, 23

K
knife mixing 53
knife painting 98-9, 117, 129

L
landscape
   hills and mountains 156-7
   people in 186-7
   trees 152-5
   tutorial: mixing acrylic and oil 162-5
   water 158-61
lemon yellow 50, 51, 52, 54
light 172, 173
light emerald green 56, 57, 64
light portrait pink 65
line and wash 134-5

M
masking 82, 83, 85, 126-9
masonite 84
medium magenta 56
mixing
   acrylic and oil 162-6
   browns and grays 64-5
   by glazing 56-7
   colorful neutrals 55
   greens 62-3
   on the palette 53, 53
modeling pastes 21, 21, 86, 118
modifying colors 54, 54
modifying hues 55, 55
monoprint 130-33

single-stage print 130-31
three-stage print 132-3
mountains see hills and
mountains
mouth diffuser 119, 140

N

naphthol crimson 54, 56, 58, 64
Naples yellow hue 62, 63
neutral colors 54, 55
nylon brushes 14, 73, 79

O

oil and acrylic 142-3
oil bars 122, 124, 125
oil pastels 122, 125, 136-9, 149, 157
oil-paint effects 30
optical mixing 45
overlaying colors 50, 50

P

paint
acrylic see acrylics
extruded paint 100-103
fabric 161
flow-formula 11, 26
full-bodied 11
gouache 146, 147
medium consistency paint
on paper 72-3
thick 28-9, 91
thick paint on canvas 74-5
thin 26-7
thin/thick contrast 31
transparent paint on paper
76-7
water-thinned 72, 73, 74, 90, 136
paint charts 49
paint pots 11
paint scraper 110, 111

paint shapers 16
chiseled 16, 17
flat 16, 16, 17
pointed 16, 17
round 16
painting knives 16, 16, 90, 106
painting mediums 20-23
acrylic modeling paste 23
the effects of mediums 21
heavy gel mediums 20, 20, 22, 22, 28
interference colors 23, 24, 24
iridescent medium 22, 23
modeling pastes 21, 21
retarding medium 20, 20, 22, 78, 79
texture pastes 21, 21, 23
painting sets 10
palette
a limited 60-61, 180-83
mixing on the 53, 53
palette knife 15, 16, 16, 53, 53, 118
palettes 18-19
improvised 18
making a stay-wet palette 19
materials 18
spraying 18
stay-wet 18, 53
tear-off 19
paper
blotting 19
drawing 19, 130
Hokai 157
medium consistency
paint on 72-3
stretching 38-9
tissue 149, 177
tracing 19
transparent paint on 76-7
watercolor 72, 114, 122, 161, 177

waxed stencil 104
pastels, oil 122, 125, 152, 157
mixing acrylic and oil 162-5
pastel and acrylic 136-9
Payne's gray 49, 52, 56, 58, 60, 61, 63, 133
pencil drawings 70, 70, 71
pencil and acrylic 144-5
pens 134, 135
people
in landscape 186-7
portraits 184-5
permanent deep green 57
permanent light blue 60, 61, 62, 65
permanent rose 51
permanent soap green 64
phthalo blue 48, 52, 56, 60, 61, 63
phthalo green 49, 54, 56, 63
piping bag 100, 101, 103
plant spray 82
plastic card 110, 111, 112
Pointillism 45
portraits 184-5
head and shoulders portraits
185
heightened colors 185
painting children 184
primary colors
creating secondaries 42
mixing tertiaries 42
primary choices 43
priming 36, 37

R

raw sienna 65
raw umber 49, 50, 52, 54, 56, 64, 65
red-violet 55
reflections 95, 158-61, 182
retarding medium 20, 20, 22, 78, 79, 92, 93, 107, 159, 184

S

sand
  making texture 28, 29
  texture pastes 21, 21
sandpaper 36
sawdust 28
scarlet red 64
scrapers 91
scraping 110-113
scumbling 28, 84-5, 88, 149, 157, 163
secondary colors 42, 43
sgraffito 91, 99, 106-9
shapes and textures 174-5
  exploring shapes 175
  fruit textures 175
  surface pattern 174
skin tones 59
soft brushes 73, 80, 86, 94
spattering 82-3
sponges 91
spraying
  acrylic ink 119
  charcoal and acrylic 140, 141
  and spattering 82
  and wet-in-wet 92
staining 37
stencil brush 104, 105
stenciling 104-5
still life 174-83
  floral groups 176-9
  shapes and textures 174-5
  tutorial: using a restricted palette 180-83
stretching canvas 34-5
stretching paper 38-9
students' colors 10
surface pattern 174

T

tertiary colors 42
textures

fruit 175
  making 28, 29
  mediums 29
  painting 171
  pastes 21, 21, 23
  shapes and textures 174-5
  texturing the surface 118-21
thick paint 28-9
  blending 28
  broken color 28
  direct painting 28
  fork 29
  making texture 29
  scumbling 28
  texture mediums 29
tin foil 29
thin paint 26-7
  adding white 27
  dark over light 27
  glazing 27
  graded wash 27
  granulation 27
  painting in watercolor mode 26, 26
  tin foil 29
titanium white 48, 52, 58, 60, 61
tonal underpainting 96-7
toothbrush 82, 83
transparency 72, 75
trees 152-5
  creating impressions 155
  descriptive paint 155
  first-hand observation 154
  framing a view 152
  soft effects 153
tube sizes 11
turquoise green 63

U

ultramarine blue 48, 50, 52, 54, 62, 65
unbleached titanium 56

underdrawing 70-71
underpainting, tonal 96-7
urban scenes 166-9
  atmosphere 168
  cityscapes 169
  landscape features 167
  modern buildings 167
  photographic realism 166

V

varnishing 21
viridian hue 64

W

washes
  graded 27
  thin 26
  transparent 72, 73, 114
  watercolor 146
water 158-61
  creating movement 158
  descriptive marks 161
  foregrounds 160
  mixing media 159
  simplification 159
watercolor 161
  watercolor and acrylic 146-7
  watercolor-style 70, 77, 92
wax resist 122-5, 149
wet-in-wet 31, 46, 92-3
  combining methods 93
  and retarding medium 20, 22
white 58, 94
  adding 27
  highlight 26
Windsor violet 51

Y

yellow ocher 48, 50, 58
yellow oxide 58, 59, 60, 61, 62, 63

Credits

While every effort has been made to credit
contributors, Quarto would like to apologize
should there have been any omissions or errors
—and would be pleased to make the
appropriate correction for future editions
of the book.